EVERYTHING YOU NEED TO KNOW TO EVALUATE A WHOLE LANGUAGE PROGRAM

Forms, Strategies, Techniques, & More

by Judith Cochran

Incentive Publications, Inc.
Nashville, Tennessee

Illustrated by Kathleen Bullock
Cover by Becky Rüegger
Edited by Leslie Britt

Library of Congress Catalog Card Number: 94-75264
ISBN 0-86530-290-1

PRINTED IN THE UNITED STATES OF AMERICA

Table of Contents

OVERVIEW

Everything You Need to Know to Evaluate a Whole Language Program seeks to provide teachers with an effective method of assessing student progress in the K-6 whole language classroom. The book examines assessment methods at the classroom, school, and district levels and covers the use of both process-oriented and standardized testing methods.

Current assessment theory is successfully combined with practical tools and strategies for immediate use in the classroom. Ready-to-reproduce-and-use assessment and record-keeping forms are included for each evaluative method in order to help teachers implement the outlined assessment strategies in their own classrooms. Chapters cover a wide variety of topics related to assessment in a whole language program: valid forms of whole language evaluation; how to effectively use standardized testing practices in a whole language program; establishing minimum standards and methods of evaluating them; administering and evaluating informal assessments; maintaining portfolios as an assessment tool; observation and notation in the classroom; methods of administering and evaluating reading records; conferencing; performance assessment; and suggestions for including parents in the evaluation process. A detailed bibliography of related materials is also included.

As in its companion book *Everything You Need To Know To Be a Successful Whole Language Teacher,* the activities and evaluative strategies in this book are categorized according to level of difficulty: emergent learners (grades K–1), developing learners (grades 2–3), and fluent learners (grades 4–6). The sample forms provided can help teachers build the foundation of their own whole language assessment programs.

Evaluation in a whole language classroom is an ongoing process that is embedded in all of the regular classwork students do. With *Everything You Need to Know to Evaluate a Whole Language Program,* teachers are provided with all of the information and materials needed to identify and implement classroom-based and standardized assessment techniques in any whole language classroom.

Chapter One

VALID FORMS OF WHOLE LANGUAGE EVALUATION

Evaluation in a whole language classroom is an ongoing process. It is embedded in all of the regular classwork students do. This concept represents a major shift from the traditional approach to assessment which interrupted the classroom routine to administer a standardized test.

Whole Language Classroom
Evaluation is embedded in regular classwork

Traditional Classroom
Class routine is interrupted to administer standardized tests

We now know that standardized tests provide only partial information about a student's learning process. Insight into the learning process can be achieved only by monitoring students' actual whole language classwork*. This process is known as classroom-based assessment and can assume many forms.

* For details about whole language classwork and curriculum, see **Everything You Need To Know To Be a Successful Whole Language Teacher** by Judith Cochran. Incentive Publications, Nashville, TN, 1993.

CLASSROOM-BASED ASSESSMENT

Classroom-based assessment is the most valid form of assessment of a student's learning process because it measures what the student can actually do and provides evidence of the student's achievements in the form of portfolios, observations, and reading records.

INFORMAL ASSESSMENTS

- Provide an overview of student learning

PORTFOLIOS

- Consist of collected samples of student work across the curriculum

OBSERVATIONS

- Anecdotal records of a teacher's observations of student performance in the classroom

READING RECORDS AND CONFERENCING

- Assessment and notation of individual student conferences

PERFORMANCE ASSESSMENT

- Students read and write about a book or a passage.
- Standardized books or passages can be assessed district-wide.

Students receive all information by hearing, seeing, or reading it, and they express themselves by either speaking or writing. Accordingly, classroom-based assessment evaluates student growth by the speaking and writing they do.

Receive	Express	
Hearing	Speaking	These are the best ways to evaluate a whole language program
Reading	Writing	

Thus, observation of a student's speaking and writing skills is the best way to evaluate the success of a whole language program.

The purpose of this book is to offer a comprehensive overview of all of these classroom-based assessment tools so that teachers, parents, district personnel, and the community can understand them. Emphasis is placed on simplicity so that these tools can be easily implemented in any classroom.

Teachers who are using classroom-based assessments for the first time should begin slowly, choosing one form of assessment that best fits into their teaching style and using it until it becomes a comfortable and natural part of their assessment programs. Other methods can then be added gradually.

Choose One To Start

To begin, choose one form of assessment and use it until it is comfortable, then gradually add another.

STANDARDIZED ASSESSMENT

Since schools and districts need to plot student progress on a broader scale than do individual teachers, they need forms of assessment that are more standardized in nature. In other words, school-wide or district assessments should be able to be administered in a similar format and manner and held to a common set of criteria. This can be accomplished two ways: semi-standardized and fully standardized assessment. In *semi-standardized assessment*, criteria is set, administered, and scored at the district level. In *fully standardized assessment*, norms are set nationally and scored at national computer scoring centers.

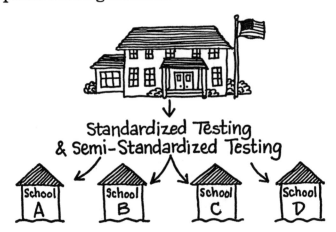

Districts need a standardized method of assessing all students to ascertain growth on a large scale.

SEMI-STANDARDIZED

Performance Assessment
- Format can be standardized and assessed district-wide.
- This form of assessment gives teachers, parents, and school or district personnel important information about student learning and progress.

Minimum Standards
- Minimum standards express minimum learning expectations for students at each grade level, K-6.
- This form of assessment provides parents, students, and the community with easily-understood parameters.

FULLY STANDARDIZED

Standardized Tests
- Standardized tests provide school and district ranking on national norms.
- This form of assessment identifies students and schools for categorical funds.

SCOPE AND SEQUENCE OF WHOLE LANGUAGE SKILLS

With the wide range of assessment needs of teachers and districts, how can a balance among all of the different methods of assessment be achieved? This is best accomplished by first adopting an overall view of the whole language skills, concepts, and experiences all students should attain. The *Scope and Sequence Chart of Whole Language Skills,* outlined on pages 13 and 14, provides a sound foundation on which teachers and district personnel can base their programs.

This scope and sequence chart divides students between the grades of kindergarten and sixth grades into three distinct groups of learners: emergent, developing, and fluent. Each group is at a different developmental stage of acquiring knowledge.

EMERGENT LEARNERS (Approximately Grades K-1)
These students are acquiring the basic skills necessary to understand the processes of reading, writing, and mathematics.

DEVELOPING LEARNERS (Approximately Grades 2-3)
These students have mastered the basic skills and can apply them in more complex ways.

FLUENT LEARNERS (Approximately Grades 4-6)
Fluent learners are well-versed in reading, writing, and mathematics skills. They are learning strategic ways to approach and use these skills in a variety of situations.

SCOPE AND SEQUENCE CHART OF WHOLE LANGUAGE SKILLS, K-6

Grades	Emerging		Developing		Fluent		
	K	1	2	3	4	5	6

LISTENING

	K	1	2	3	4	5	6
Students Listen as Teacher Reads Aloud Daily	x	x	x	x	x	x	x
Students Have Daily Opportunities To Listen	x	x	x	x	x	x	x

SPEAKING

	K	1	2	3	4	5	6
Students Have Daily Opportunities To Speak	x	x	x	x	x	x	x

READING

	K	1	2	3	4	5	6
Teacher Reads Aloud Daily	x	x	x	x	x	x	x
Students Read Silently Every Day	x	x	x	x	x	x	x
Students Read in Other Situations Daily	x	x	x	x	x	x	x
Word Identification							
• phonics (vowels/consonants)	x	x	x				
• contractions, compound words		x	x	x			
• sight words		x	x	x			
Vocabulary							
• recognize word meanings	x	x	x	x	x	x	x
• roots, prefixes, suffixes	x	x	x	x	x	x	x
• synonyms/antonyms	x	x	x	x	x	x	x
• unfamiliar words in context	x	x	x	x	x	x	x
Comprehension							
Literal							
• details	x	x	x	x	x	x	x
• pronoun reference	x	x	x	x	x	x	x
• sequence	x	x	x	x	x	x	x
Inferential							
• relate story to personal experiences	x	x	x	x	x	x	x
• main idea	x	x	x	x	x	x	x
• cause/effect	x	x	x	x	x	x	x
• draw conclusions	x	x	x	x	x	x	x

READING (Continued)

Emerging   Developing   Fluent

Grades	K	1	2	3	4	5	6
• predict outcomes	X	X	X	X	X	X	X
• compare/contrast	X	X	X	X	X	X	X
Critical Thinking							
• analyze character, setting	X	X	X	X	X	X	X
• real/make-believe		X	X	X			
• summarize plot			X	X	X	X	X
• fact/opinion					X	X	X
• mood						X	X
• author's tone/intent						X	X
Study Skills							
• maps/charts/graphs	X	X	X	X	X	X	X
• book parts (table of contents/title page/index)	X	X	X	X	X	X	X
• alphabetization			X	X			
• dictionary			X	X	X	X	X
• reference (newspaper/telephone book/ encyclopedia/atlas)			X	X	X	X	X
• card catalog				X	X	X	X

WRITING

Grades	K	1	2	3	4	5	6
Students Write Every Day journal/informal/formal writing experiences	X	X	X	X	X	X	X
Spelling							
• invented	X	X	X	X			
• formal		X	X	X	X	X	X
Sentences/Paragraphs							
• teacher writes dictated sentences	X	X	X				
• students complete sentence/story frames	X	X	X				
• write original sentences/paragraphs		X	X	X	X	X	X
• use vivid words (adjectives/adverbs/verbs)		X	X	X	X	X	X
• capitalization/punctuation/grammar		X	X	X	X	X	X
• letter form (personal/business)		X	X	X	X	X	X
• poetry		X	X	X	X	X	X
• organize information for paragraphs/reports			X	X	X	X	X

*From *Everything You Need To Know To Be A Successful Whole Language Teacher* by Judith Cochran. Nashville, TN: Incentive Publications, 1993. Used by permission.

A BALANCED APPROACH TO EVALUATION

There exists a need to use assessments that provide teachers, parents, school and district personnel, and the community with the information they need to assess student growth. This can be done by instituting a balanced approach to evaluation. Common sense dictates that both classroom-based assessments and standardized assessments should be used to evaluate whole language programs.

The chart below illustrates who benefits from the information revealed in each type of assessment, and can also be used to determine the type of assessment to use in a variety of situations. For example, since teachers are in daily contact with the student, classroom-based assessments should be given as much emphasis as standardized assessments.

CLASSROOM-BASED	Teachers	Parents	District	Community
Informal Assessment	X	X		
Portfolios	X	X	X	
Observation	X	X		
Reading Records and Conferences	X	X	X	
STANDARDIZED ASSESSMENT				
Performance Assessments	X	X	X	X
Minimum Standards	X	X	X	X
Standardized Tests*	X	X	X	X

Do not place undue attention on standardized test scores. Everyone involved should view the results as only a part of the whole picture of student assessment.

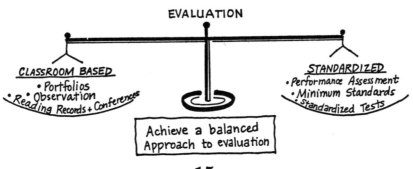

Chapter Two

HOW TO USE STANDARDIZED TESTING IN A WHOLE LANGUAGE PROGRAM

We have seen how a combination of classroom-based and standardized tests are necessary for a balanced approach to whole language evaluation. This chapter will analyze the forms of standardized testing currently being used in the classroom and show the whole language teacher how to best implement this type of assessment in a whole language program.

For the purposes of this book, two types of standardized testing have been identified:

• Semi-Standardized
Standards and criteria for this form of assessment are set at the district level. These tests are assessed, administered, and scored district-wide. This type of assessment includes performance assessment and minimum standards for each grade level.

• Fully Standardized
Standards and norms are set nationally. Tests are scored at national computer scoring centers. These evaluations include such tests as the CTBS and SAT.

Evaluating a whole language program with standardized assessment tools presents special problems. Because whole language classrooms immerse the students in all aspects of reading, writing, listening, and speaking, the information standardized tests offer have little relevance. Multiple choice formats offer an especially limited view of students' learning.

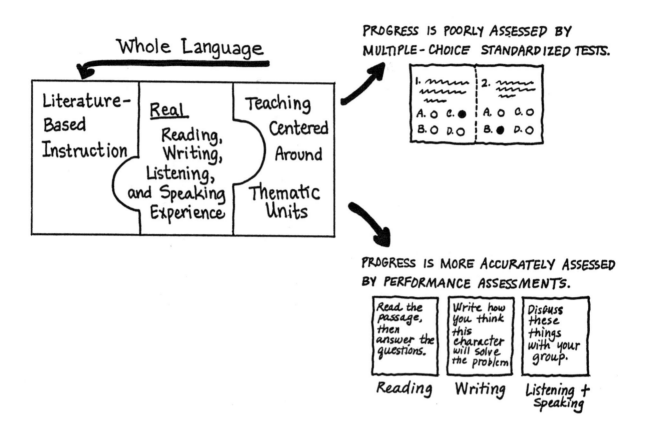

Semi-standardized assessments, however, can present a fine balance between teacher and district assessment needs.

SEMI-STANDARDIZED ASSESSMENT

Performance assessments require students to write a response to questions about a book or a passage. At the district level, an appropriate book or passage is chosen for each grade level, and a set of standard questions and procedures are established for the teacher and students to follow (see Chapter 8, pages 111–144, for more specific information on performance assessments). Student responses are scored at the district level depending on the learning level of the students (emergent learners' work will be scored at the school sites). Because performance assessments closely resemble regular classwork, they are the best standardized tests to use to assess the full spectrum of a student's learning.

Minimum standards set for each grade level also provide important information at the classroom and district levels. These standards are best assessed through a body of student work collected throughout the year. (For more information on setting minimum standards, see Chapter 3, pages 23–36.)

In the last thirty years, the use of fully standardized tests has increased dramatically. School districts administer these tests to ascertain student progress, basal reading programs use them to evaluate which students should progress to the next level of learning, and the federal government requires them to qualify for categorical funds. District administrators and school boards also use standardized tests to judge the effectiveness of principals and their schools' reading and math programs. In fact, these tests are used to assess many elements they were not originally intended to assess. Standardized tests were originally designed to provide a general assessment of reading and math abilities by using a uniformly administered and scored test. They have recently become the only measurement of student progress considered in most school districts.

Use standardized tests as overview of Reading/Math Skills Only

OVERVIEW

Reading ..... 85th percentile

Math Computation .... 90th percentile

Math Application ... 87th percentile

DO NOT USE STANDARDIZED TESTS ......

...to judge site principal effectiveness

OR

...as the only measure of student progress

PROS AND CONS OF STANDARDIZED TESTS

Standardized tests are not all bad. They provide a partial assessment of reading and math abilities quickly and cheaply. Norm-referenced tests provide percentile rankings which help schools identify exceptional students: those who are gifted, have learning disabilities, or qualify for other district, state, or federal programs. Standardized test scores also give school boards and communities a general indication of how their district ranks when compared with others across the nation. However, standardized tests do not measure everything a child needs to be proficient in reading. Nor do they take into account individual differences in background or experience, or take into consideration the critical interplay of reading and writing skills, thus missing the point of whole language.

We know these things about fully standardized tests and their results:

- Students do poorly when they are not familiar with the topics of test passages.

- "Test wise" students do well, but may test higher in reading than their abilities actually warrant.

- Standardized question formats do not allow students to use strategies they need for real-life reading situations.

Fully standardized testing has affected classroom reading programs in ways never intended. The more teacher accountability becomes linked to increasing standardized test scores, the greater the focus on low level reading skills that are easily tested. This overemphasis can account for more time spent on worksheets that provide practice in the mundane skills needed to pass the test. When these flaws are combined with the misuse of standardized test scores, it is clear that a complete reliance on fully standardized testing is inappropriate and unfair to students.

However, when standardized tests are considered as only one indication of student performance, a balanced and complete whole language program can emerge. When this happens, teachers find that the scores on standardized tests generally confirm their own conclusions about student abilities.

An overemphasis on standardized test results causes teachers to spend more time on low-level reading skills assessed best by mundane worksheets.

When standardized test results are seen as <u>one</u> <u>indicator</u> of student progress, the scores confirm teacher's knowledge about the child.

RECOMMENDATIONS FOR BALANCED STANDARDIZED TESTING PRACTICES

A balanced approach to standardized testing needs to be adopted in order to synthesize national, district, and classroom information about student learning. This could include yearly assessment with a fully standardized test, administering only three sub-tests: reading comprehension, math computation, and math applications.

Performance assessments can be given two or three times a school year to assess progress in concepts outlined on the *Scope and Sequence Chart of Whole Language Skills,* on pages 13–14. Performance assessment can also determine if minimum standards have been met.

STANDARDIZED TEST ADMINISTRATION

	Subtests	How Often
Fully Standardized Tests (CTBS, SAT, CAT, etc.)	**Reading Comprehension Math Computation Math Applications**	**Yearly***
Semi-standardized Tests: Performance Assessment	**Concepts outlined on Scope & Sequence Chart of Whole Language Skills, pages 13-14**	**2–3 times a year**
Minimum Standards	**All district-determined minimums**	**When performance assessment is given, or when body of student work indicates standards are met**

Twice a year if necessary to qualify for categorical funding

When considering the use of standardized tests in the whole language classroom, remember that the teacher/student relationship should center on real teaching and learning processes and not the continued burden of formal testing. In a whole language classroom, the actual classwork students produce best reflects what is being learned.

Chapter Three

SETTING MINIMUM STANDARDS

Setting minimum standards at the district level helps everyone concerned with a child's education—teachers, parents, district personnel—understand what every student will know before passing to the next grade level. Minimum standards define parameters that the students and community at large can understand as well.

Minimums are by no means the average or desirable expectations of each grade level. They merely establish a grade's basic level of knowledge. Students may achieve any level of learning above this minimum standard, but should not slip below the minimum standards.

KINDERGARTEN   FIRST GRADE   SECOND GRADE   THIRD GRADE

Minimum standards establish a floor of knowledge
required for each grade level.

Teachers, parents, and district personnel need to be involved in every aspect of establishing minimum standards. The process should look something like this:

SITE INPUT
Each school submits ideas for minimums at each grade level.

DISTRICT COMMITTEE
A representative sample of teachers and principals from each grade level and socioeconomic area establishes minimums from school input.

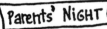

SITES DISTRIBUTE
Each school distributes minimums to parents.

SCHOOL BOARD
Minimums finalized after final input by sites, community, and district committee. School board passes establishment of minimum standards for each grade level, K-6.

COMMUNITY MEETING
District committee meets with community members representing each grade level and socioeconomic area to communicate minimums and receive input.

EXAMPLES OF MINIMUMS FOR EACH GRADE LEVEL

Listed below are examples of minimum standards for each grade level. Keep in mind the broad scope of a whole language program; often minimums for one grade level are the standard expectations for the previous grade level.

LANGUAGE ARTS

Listening/Speaking
- Listens to stories and comments and/or asks questions about them
- Expresses self in sentences

Reading
- Spends time looking through books on a daily basis
- Points to words in text
- Knows most letter names and sounds
- Relates story details

Writing
- Writes most letters by name and sound
- Attempts to write words with correct beginning sounds

MATH

Numbers/Numeration
- Counts, identifies, and writes numbers to 10
- Matches objects with numbers 1 through 10
- Classifies objects using one attribute

Geometry
- Identifies basic geometric shapes

Measurement
- Identifies long/longer/longest and short/shorter/shortest

Problem-Solving
- Completes simple shape pattern

LANGUAGE ARTS

Listening/Speaking
- Communicates well in small group and sharing activities
- Listens to stories and comments, asks questions about, or retells them
- Relates story to personal experiences

Reading
- Reads predictable books with a repeated rhyme or pattern and can point to the words
- Knows letter names and sounds, and makes an attempt to decode phonetic words
- Relates story details
- Participates in silent reading daily
- Sequences beginning/ending of story
- Predicts what will happen next in the story

Writing
- Reads own writing
- Copies from board
- Completes a simple sentence frame
- Invented spelling includes beginning and ending sounds

MATH

Numbers/Numeration
- Counts, identifies, and writes numbers to 20
- Understands before/after
- Classifies objects by two attributes

Operations
- Knows addition facts to 10
- Knows subtraction facts to 10

Geometry
- Draws basic shapes
- Understands simple symmetry

Measurement
- Measures length with non-standard unit
- Tells time to hour
- Identifies money values: 1¢, 5¢, 10¢, 25¢

Problem-Solving
- Completes shape patterns

Interpretation
- Reads simple graphs

LANGUAGE ARTS

Listening/Speaking
- Communicates well in small group and sharing activities
- Listens to stories and comments, asks questions about, or retells them
- Relates story to personal experiences

Reading
- Participates in silent reading on a daily basis
- Knows many sight words
- Predicts outcomes and draws conclusions
- Decodes unfamiliar words, phonetically or through context
- Relates story details
- Distinguishes between real/make-believe
- Sequences beginning/middle/end of story

Writing
- Reads own writing
- Writes original sentences
- Invented spelling includes beginning/middle/ending sounds
- Spells some words correctly
- Knows initial capitals and ending punctuation

MATH

Numbers/Numeration
- Counts, identifies, and writes numbers to 100
- Understands greater/less to 20
- Understands before/after to 100
- Knows ordinal numbers to 3rd
- Sequences three numbers to 20
- Counts by 5s and 10s

Operations
- Adds three numbers
- Understands addition without regrouping
- Understands subtraction without regrouping

Geometry
- Knows fractional shapes: ¼, ½
- Distinguishes between similar and basic shapes
- Understands symmetry

Measurement
- Measures length with non-standard units
- Tells time to half-hour
- Reads a calendar
- Adds money to 30¢

Problem-Solving
- Completes shape patterns
- Completes simple number patterns
- Computes orally-given word problems
- Uses simple number sentences to solve oral word problems

Interpretation
- Interprets simple graphs and charts

LANGUAGE ARTS

Listening/Speaking
- Communicates well in small/large group and sharing activities
- Listens to stories and comments, asks questions about, or retells them
- Relates story to personal experiences

Reading
- Participates in silent reading on a daily basis
- Has large sight-word vocabulary
- Has good word attack skills using context clues
- Relates and sequences story details and events
- Predicts outcomes and draws conclusions
- Understands main idea
- Understands cause/effect relationships

Writing
- Writes a simple paragraph
- Spells many words correctly
- Few capitalization/punctuation errors
- Writes to topic

MATH

Numbers/Numeration
- Knows place value to 100s
- Knows ordinal numbers to 10th
- Understands greater/less to 100
- Understands before/after to 100
- Sequences numbers to 100

Operations
- Knows addition with regrouping
- Knows subtraction with regrouping
- Knows multiplication facts to 5

Geometry
- Knows fractional shapes: ¼, ⅓, ½
- Distinguishes between similar shapes
- Knows 2- and 3-dimensional shapes
- Understands symmetry
- Distinguishes between equivalent shapes

Measurement
- Measures in inches
- Tells time to a quarter of an hour
- Reads a calendar

Problem Solving
- Writes number sentences
- Sees number patterns
- Solves word problems
- Solves equivalent equations

Interpretation
- Interprets graphs/charts
- Reads maps

FAIRY TALE

28

LANGUAGE ARTS

Listening/Speaking
- Communicates well in small/large group and sharing activities
- Relates story to personal experiences

Reading
- Participates in silent reading on a daily basis
- Self-corrects and uses context clues with unfamiliar words
- Compares and contrasts characters
- Understands cause/effect relationships
- Predicts outcomes and draws conclusions
- Understands main idea
- Comprehends simple plot summary

Writing
- Uses paragraph form and writes to topic
- Uses vivid words in writing
- Uses correct capitalization/ punctuation
- Writes with few grammatical errors
- Correctly spells most common words

MATH

Numbers/Numeration
- Knows place value to 1000s
- Understands before/after, greater/less to 1000
- Understands even/odd numbers
- <, >, =

Operations
- Knows addition/subtraction with regrouping
- Knows multiplication without regrouping
- Can add/subtract money problems
- Knows division facts to 9

Geometry
- Knows fractional shapes: ⅛, ¼, ⅓, ½
- Knows 2- and 3-dimensional shapes
- Understands symmetry
- Distinguishes between equivalent shapes
- Understands the concept of congruence
- Knows perimeter/area

Measurement
- Measures in inches: ½ inch, ¼ inch
- Measures in centimeters
- Tells time to 5 minutes
- Accurately reads a calendar
- Knows capacity (pint, quart, gallon)
- Reads a thermometer

Problem-Solving
- Sees number patterns
- Solves word problems
- Understands number sentences
- Solves equivalent equations
- Estimates

Interpretation
- Interprets tables/graphs/charts
- Reads maps

LANGUAGE ARTS

Listening/Speaking
- Communicates well in small/large group and sharing activities
- Relates reading to personal experiences

Reading
- Participates in silent reading on a daily basis
- Analyzes character and setting
- Identifies fact/opinion
- Compares and contrasts characters
- Understands cause/effect relationships
- Predicts outcomes and draws conclusions
- Understands main idea
- Summarizes plot

Writing
- Organizes information into paragraphs
- Uses vivid words in writing
- Writes a personal letter
- Understands and writes poetry
- Uses conventional spelling most of the time
- Uses reference materials
- Uses correct capitalization/punctuation/grammar

MATH

Numbers/Numeration
- Sequences numbers to 1000
- Understands even/odd numbers
- $<, >, =$
- Knows simple Roman numerals

Operations
- Adds/subtracts decimals and money
- Knows multiplication with regrouping
- Adds/subtracts simple fractions
- Knows division with remainders

Geometry
- Knows equivalent fractions
- Knows 2- and 3-dimensional shapes
- Identifies figures
- Distinguishes between equivalent shapes
- Understands the concept of congruence
- Knows perimeter/area/volume
- Understands coordinates (graphing)

Measurement
- Measures in inches/feet/yards
- Measures in centimeters/meters
- Tells correct time
- Knows calendar conversions (day, week, month)
- Knows capacity (cup, pint, quart, gallon)
- Reads a thermometer (Fahrenheit and Celsius)

Problem-Solving
- Sees number patterns
- Solves word problems (including money problems)
- Understands number sentences
- Solves equivalent equations
- Estimates

Interpretation
- Interprets tables/graphs/charts
- Reads maps/diagrams

LANGUAGE ARTS

Listening/Speaking
- Communicates well in small/large group and sharing activities
- Relates reading to personal experiences

Reading
- Participates in silent reading on a daily basis
- Analyzes character and setting
- Identifies fact/opinion
- Compares and contrasts characters
- Understands cause/effect relationships
- Predicts outcomes and draws conclusions
- Understands main idea
- Summarizes plot
- Understands mood and author's tone and intent

Writing
- Organizes information into paragraphs and reports
- Uses vivid words in writing
- Writes a personal letter
- Understands and writes poetry
- Consistently uses conventional spelling
- Uses reference materials
- Uses correct capitalization/ punctuation/grammar

MATH

Numbers/Numeration
- Sequences numbers
- Understands even/odd numbers
- <, >, =
- Knows Roman numerals

Operations
- Adds/subtracts/multiplies/divides decimals
- Adds/subtracts/multiplies fractions
- Knows division with remainders
- Converts fractions to decimals

Geometry
- Identifies figures/angles
- Knows 2- and 3-dimensional shapes
- Measures circle parts (radius, diameter, circumference)
- Distinguishes between equivalent shapes
- Understands the concept of congruence
- Knows perimeter/area/volume
- Understands coordinates (graphing)

Measurement
- Measures in inches/feet/yards
- Measures in centimeters/meters
- Knows when to use the appropriate standard of measure
- Tells time, uses a calendar, reads a thermometer
- Knows capacity (cup, pint, quart, gallon)
- Converts standard measuring units

Problem-Solving
- Sees number patterns
- Solves word problems (including money problems)
- Understands number sentences
- Solves equivalent equations
- Estimates

Interpretation
- Interprets tables/graphs/charts
- Reads maps/diagrams

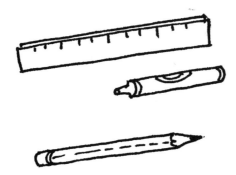

Note that the subject areas of Science and Social Studies are not included in the minimums standards. This is because it is assumed that much of the reading, writing, and math skills will be organized around central themes found in the sciences and social studies.

Again, minimum standards are not the typical expectations teachers should hold for each grade level. They are only guarantees to students, parents, and the community that students at each grade level will have a common understanding of these concepts when entering the next grade level. Many school districts establish regular expectations as well as minimums. These outline what the majority of students should learn before passing on to the next grade.

EVALUATING MINIMUM STANDARDS

It is up to each school district to decide the method of evaluating or determining a passing grade or minimum standards. This can be done a number of ways:

1. Review of a Body of Student Work
   - portfolios (including writing profiles and math continuums)
     - informal assessments
     - reading records

2. Performance Assessment

3. Standardized Tests

Each of these means of evaluations is examined in detail below.

A BODY OF STUDENT WORK

Most teachers have maintained portfolios for years. Portfolios are folders containing samples of student work that chart progress over the year. Reproducible portfolio forms, reading records, and conferencing forms which include minimum standards have been included in Chapter 5, pages 45-75, and Chapter 7, pages 83–110.

Informal assessments (see Chapter 4, pages 37–43) can also serve as a way to successfully evaluate minimum standards in math and in some reading and writing skills. Because informal assessment is short by nature, it lends itself to skills that can be illustrated quickly and in a short form. Skills such as the math operations of addition, subtraction, multiplication, and division can be assessed by working a few problems. In the area of reading, specific details of a story or the sequencing of events can be demonstrated easily within the format of the informal assessment. Spelling, capitalization, and punctuation also are easily assessed by this format. However, the more complex concepts involved in reading comprehension and written expression are better assessed through collections in portfolios or performance assessments.

Portfolios
A collection of student work through the year can show that a student meets all minimum standards.

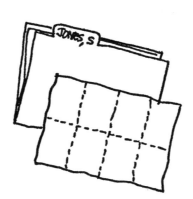

Informal Assessment
Most math minimums can be demonstrated this way, but complex reading and writing concepts require other forms of assessment.

Observation
Listening and speaking abilities are best assessed this way.

Observation is the best way to assess a student's listening and speaking abilities. It is also the only way to determine whether a student is participating in silent reading every day.

All in all, a body of student work is the best and most desirable way to assess and evaluate established minimum standards in a whole language program. The next best way is through performance assessment.

PERFORMANCE ASSESSMENT

Performance assessment is a formalized method of asking students to respond to a book or written passage in writing. A performance assessment usually stresses the more complex reading comprehension skills of character analysis and predicting outcomes. It is a very reliable source of whole language evaluation since it employs the same techniques students have been using with all their lessons: reading, writing, listening, and speaking.

To score performance assessments, teachers throughout the district meet and score each student's work according to an established rubric of attributes for the particular grade level. A minimum score can be established for a child to be considered to have passed the minimum standards.

Performance Assessment
Asks students to do the same kind of reading, writing, listening and speaking they normally do in the classroom

Scoring Rubric
Scored by grade-level teachers at district level

Predetermined Score
A predetermined score is needed to pass minimum standards and move to next grade level.

Performance assessment is an excellent way to evaluate all aspects of minimum standards in language arts. A form of performance assessment can also be used to assess math concepts. For more information, see Chapter 8, pages 111–144.

STANDARDIZED TESTS

Although a standardized test can be used to decide if students have met minimum standards, it is not the most desirable means for doing so. The information that students can express verbally or in writing through a body of classwork or a performance assessment is reduced to filling in the correct bubble on a standardized test. The more complex reading, writing, and math concepts cannot be accurately assessed this way.

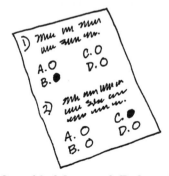

One-sided Approach To Learning
Multiple choice format provides limited access to the scope of a student's learning.

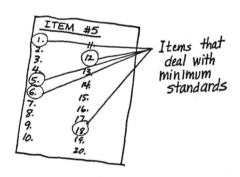

Scoring Minimum Items
Computerized scoring can be programmed to scan for specific items determined to test minimum standards.

While it can be time-consuming and moderately expensive, standardized tests can be scored for specific items predetermined by district personnel to test specific minimum standards. The score received for each student will show the regular test results along with an indication of which minimum items were missed or correct.

A problem inherent in this process is the limited number of items used to test each particular concept. Students can be judged as having passed or failed a minimum standard based on their answers to one question. All of the research supporting the whole language movement proves the limitation of this form of assessment. If this form of standardized testing is used at all, the results should be taken as only one indication of a child's learning.

Chapter Four

INFORMAL ASSESSMENT

Informal assessments are just that—a quick and informal method of assessing student learning. They can be used in the classroom in three ways:

- Weekly—Administer an informal assessment at the beginning or end of each week to serve as an overview of the skills which students have internalized or with which they still need help.

- Filler—Use an informal assessment as a ten-or fifteen-minute activity in between scheduled activities.

- Follow-up—Give an informal assessment after a completed unit of study to ascertain what was learned, retained, or appreciated the most.

How and when informal assessments are used is entirely up to the teacher and will vary according to the instructor's needs.

METHODS OF ADMINISTERING INFORMAL ASSESSMENT

The quickest and easiest way to administer an informal assessment is to give students paper (either blank or lined), and to instruct them to fold their papers into fourths or eighths and number the boxes accordingly. Then give students the information to draw, write, or compute in each box.

Fold Paper
Lined or plain paper is folded into fourths or eighths.

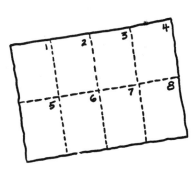

Number Each Box
Students number each box on their paper. (NOTE: Emergent learners should start with 2 to 4 boxes.)

Follow Teacher Directions
Students draw, write, or compute what teacher directs in each box.

Each step in this process not only helps the teacher assess what the students have learned, but also provides the teacher with insight into the students' listening skills. An informal assessment should not be viewed in the same way as a pop quiz, however. The informal assessment is intended for the teacher's information only and helps him or her decide how to proceed with instruction—when to review and when to introduce new concepts.

EVALUATING INFORMAL ASSESSMENTS

To assist with evaluating informal assessments, two forms are included at the end of this chapter: the *Small Group Activity* form on page 42 and the *Individual Informal Assessment Results* form on page 43. These forms were designed to help the teacher with record keeping. The *Small Group Activity* form allows teachers to record notes on concepts and activities in which small groups of students need reinforcement. The *Individual Informal Assessment Results* form allows teachers to record notes and comments on specific concepts in which a student needs reinforcement.

FILING INFORMAL ASSESSMENTS

Informal assessments, the *Small Group Activity* form, and the *Individual Informal Assessment Results* form can be filed in this manner:

Student Portfolio
File periodically in student's portfolio containing other classwork in the areas of math, science, and social studies.

Teacher Anecdotal Files
These files contain anecdotal records on students.

Refer to the *Scope and Sequence Chart of Whole Language Skills* on pages 13–14 and Chapter 3, "Setting Minimum Standards," pages 23–36 as guides to appropriate skills and concepts for each grade level. The informal assessment is one way to ascertain when students have achieved the minimum standards set for them. The *Scope and Sequence Chart of Whole Language Skills*, the Individual Writing Profiles, pages 60–65, and Math Continuum forms, pages 69–75 also outline skills and concepts appropriate to each developmental and grade level. These forms can serve as guidelines when seeking answers to questions about informal assessments.

The evaluation should be written in the corresponding boxes on the student's paper. It is important that each evaluation be dated in order to accurately track student growth. The assessment can then be filed in either the student's math, science, or social studies folder, or in an anecdotal folder which is kept for each student (see Chapter 5, "Portfolios," pages 45-76, for further details.)

To prescribe activities according to the needs revealed in the informal assessment, a *Small Group Activity* Sheet is provided on page 42. On it, a teacher lists the names of students in his or her class, writes comments, and then decides on small group activities for specific students or the entire class. This form helps the teacher identify students who need help with a particular concept, or who are ready to move on to the next skill level.

Example:

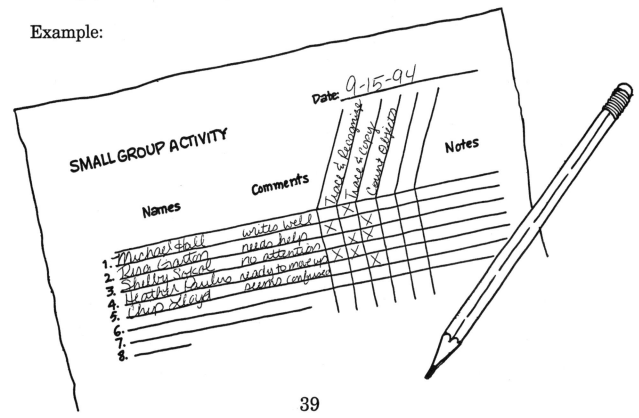

If informal assessments are administered weekly, the information they provide can help the teacher organize small group instruction for the upcoming week.

Teacher Works With Group
Teacher calls up students who need work on specific skills.

Group Rotations
Groups of students rotate to work on the specific skills outlined on the informal assessment.

Another form teachers may find useful is the *Individual Informal Assessment Results* form on page 43. On it, teachers can record a year's worth of significant informal assessment results on one page. This form can be shown to parents during a parent-teacher conference to help them track their child's progress. It can also be shown to an administrator or the principal as a representation of the entire body of a student's work.

EMERGENT LEARNERS (Grades K-1)

Since students at this level are just beginning to understand the basic tenets of reading, writing, and mathematics, they should be asked to draw their responses to the teacher's informal assessment questions. However, they should be encouraged to describe their pictures in writing since these early attempts at writing provide insight into each child's understanding of the connection between spoken and written language. It is recommended that emergent learners in kindergarten and the beginning of first grade begin participating in informal assessment by using only two or four boxes per evaluation.

DEVELOPING LEARNERS (Grades 2–3)

Developing learners have mastered basic skills and are able to reason and solve problems. These children are able to supply written answers and can handle informal assessments with eight boxes.

FLUENT LEARNERS (Grades 4–6)

Fluent learners have mastered reading, writing, and mathematical skills, and they are using these skills to think critically about larger concepts. Students at this level should often be asked to substantiate their thinking process and should not be bound to formats that stress right or wrong answers. The informal assessment is an excellent way to evaluate fluent learners' skills so that they can spend the bulk of their time on the higher processes of thinking.

Write everything you know about finding the area of a rectangle.

The informal assessment provides a quick and easy way for teachers to ascertain the skills their students have learned and those on which they need more work. When used periodically, the informal assessment can give parents a good overview of their child's skill level and progress in the classroom. When used on a weekly basis, the information can be used to group students and prepare for the following week's instruction. No matter how it is used, the informal assessment is an excellent way to periodically evaluate a whole language program.

SMALL GROUP ACTIVITY

Date: _____

Names	Comments							Notes
1.								
2.								
3.								
4.								
5.								
6.								
7.								
8.								
9.								
10.								
11.								
12.								
13.								
14.								
15.								
16.								
17.								
18.								
19.								
20.								
21.								
22.								
23.								
24.								
25.								
26.								
27.								
28.								
29.								
30.								
31.								
32.								
33.								
34.								
35.								

Student Name_____ Grade_____ Year_____

INDIVIDUAL INFORMAL ASSESSMENT RESULTS

Date   Comments

Date	Comments

Chapter Five

PORTFOLIOS

The idea of the portfolio originated with artists, photographers, and models who collect in a folder the work which best illustrates their abilities and progress. This idea is now being transferred to the whole language classroom and used as an evaluative instrument. Portfolios are one of the most important assessment tools in a whole language classroom.

When used properly, portfolios do not require an inordinate amount of teacher time or vast areas of storage space. In fact, to be most effective, portfolios need to be kept simple. A portfolio should contain only enough material to assess the growth and progress a student has achieved throughout the school year. It should not contain every piece of work the student has completed.

Maintaining portfolios should be a comfortable and manageable process for teachers. The key to this is keeping the portfolio system simple. Teachers who are trying out portfolios for the first time should ease slowly into the process by implementing just one of the types of portfolios listed below. It is also best to maintain no more than three student folders for different types of work. Anything more can become unwieldy.

FOR FILING STUDENT WORK

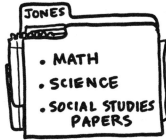

Writing Portfolio
This is the most extensive folder, containing examples of student writing completed throughout the year.

Math/Science/Social Studies
This folder contains samples of papers from these subjects completed throughout the year.

Showcase Portfolio
This folder contains examples of a student's best work across the curriculum completed throughout the year.

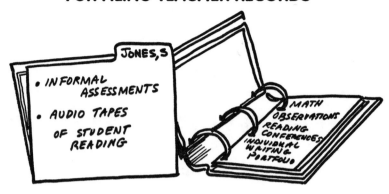

Anecdotal Records
This folder contains notations the teacher makes
regarding students and their work.

Note that only three folders contain student work. The other two portfolios contain anecdotal records kept by the teacher. All of these portfolios together represent a comprehensive, yet manageable, cross section of student work that will show progress to the student, the teacher, and the parent. The contents of each portfolio will be examined in detail on the following pages.

THE WRITING PORTFOLIO

The writing portfolio will contain the largest sample of student work completed over the course of the school year because there are many complex learning processes involved in writing. Depending on the developmental level of the students, a great deal can be learned about their listening, reading, and speaking abilities—and how they organize their ideas—simply by analyzing their writing. One of the most important aspects of maintaining a successful writing portfolio is to date each entry so that student progress can be checked over time.

Students at all levels should write every day. For those in kindergarten, this might involve nothing more than drawing a picture and "scribble writing." Although unsophisticated, this act introduces children to the writing process. For fluent learners, the writing can be in the form of letters, reports, journal entries, etc.

All of the writing students do will fall into one of three general categories: journal writing, informal writing, and formal writing.

- **Journal Writing** provides a place where students can respond to books the teacher reads aloud or that they read themselves.
  NOTE: Students can buy commercially-made booklets for their journals or they can make them themselves.

- **Informal Writing** provides a forum within which students can express themselves creatively or convey information.

- **Formal Writing** is writing intended for an audience to read and should adhere to the formal rules of writing (spelling and mechanics).

Of course, the types of activities completed in each category of writing will vary according to the developmental level of the class.

EMERGENT LEARNERS (Grades K–1)

Emergent learners are just beginning to understand the correlation between spoken and written language. Their writing is in its formative stage and will take time to develop. Even so, daily writing assignments are important for these students. Daily writing helps emergent learners view writing as a life skill, and, because reading and writing are closely related processes, daily writing reinforces developing reading skills. The writing these students complete in each of the writing categories will provide all of the information a teacher needs to successfully evaluate their abilities.

Journal Writing

Journal assignments for emergent learners should be given in response to a book the teacher reads aloud. Predictable books with repeated patterns or rhymes are best to start with at this level. Of course, teachers normally do a great deal of brainstorming, charting stories, and writing words on the board to model how to complete sentence frames, begin stories, and so on. These important techniques should also be part of every journal writing assignment.

Emergent learners' pictures and attempts at writing can be assessed in a number of areas: recalling details, sequencing events, relating the story to a personal experience, drawing conclusions, predicting outcomes, comparing/contrasting, and identifying real and make-believe events. Knowledge of grammar, spelling, and other mechanical information are also revealed in their writing. However, the need for correct spelling and mechanics in the journal assignments should not be stressed. The journal should provide a forum within which these students can express themselves and communicate ideas. Correct spelling and mechanics will be stressed during formal writing exercises.

Example:

Informal Writing

Emergent learners should also be asked to write original stories and personal experiences. These informal writing assignments allow students to express themselves in a variety of ways. The ability to compose original stories also signals to the teacher that a student has reached a new developmental level. When prewriters begin to compose their own stories, they become emergent writers. When beginning writers express themselves through a story, they become developing writers. The teacher can also assess the writer's knowledge of grammar, spelling, punctuation, and vocabulary through informal writing exercises.

Examples of each kind of story a student writes, as well as those samples showing growth in the areas of language form and usage, should be filed in the writing portfolio.

Formal Writing

Formal writing is a teacher-directed exercise intended to be read by an audience. Therefore, the writer should follow the conventional rules of spelling, grammar, and punctuation. Typically, students are taught a specific writing skill which they must then apply to the formal writing assignment. The assignments are then corrected only for the specific skill or concept being taught.

DEVELOPING LEARNERS (Grades 2–3)

Developing learners understand the basics of writing and need experiences that will enlarge their means of communication. Their everyday writing experiences are all the teacher needs to evaluate their abilities and progress.

Journal Writing

Journal assignments at this level can be given in response to books the teacher reads aloud or passages the students read themselves and discuss in small or large group situations. The journal is also the perfect outlet for brainstorming and prewriting activities.

Spelling and grammar errors should not be corrected in the journal, although the quality of a student's writing will indicate to the teacher whether certain concepts need to be reviewed. Conventional rules of spelling and grammar will be reinforced in formal writing assignments. Remember, as students write more frequently, the quality of their writing will most certainly improve.

Example:

Informal Writing

Students can express themselves informally through the writing of original stories, the writing of personal experience stories, and completing expository writing assignments. As with journal writing, correct spelling, grammar, and punctuation should not be corrected in informal writing assignments. However, an analysis of the student's writing style can tell the teacher the level at which individual students are performing in specific areas.

Examples of each type of writing the students complete should be filed along with those samples that reveal developmental growth and progress.

Formal Writing

Because formal writing assignments are intended for an audience, students need to follow the conventional rules of spelling and mechanics. Formal writing assignments should be given at least once a week, and one specific skill or concept should be stressed in each assignment. During the week following the formal writing assignment, students can be asked to apply the learned concept in their journals and informal writing assignments. The formal writing assignment should be corrected only for the skill being taught so that students may come to fully understand one concept before moving on to the next one.

Editing for Proper Spelling, Punctuation, and Grammar

Students at the developmental level (grades 2–3) should be introduced to the editing process when completing their formal writing assignments. Once a formal piece of writing has been edited, students can have their assignments "published" and placed in the class library. These published books may eventually be placed in the students' showcase portfolios.

The Editing Process

Teacher models
the editing process.

Students edit their work
together in pairs.

Note: Seeing this rough draft is evidence the student is self-editing. Mark this on the Writing Profile and file in the student's Writing Portfolio.

Student edits own
rough draft.

FLUENT LEARNERS (Grades 4–6)

Fluent learners understand the mechanics of the writing process and need practice with a variety of formats to develop fluency and the ability to organize their ideas and write to different audiences. These students need to apply writing as a life skill.

Journal Writing

The fluent learners' journal writing assignments should be stimulated by the books they are reading and the thematic units they are studying. Fluent learners should also write journal entries on a daily basis (with many other opportunities to write included in the daily schedule).

Spelling, grammar, and punctuation should not be stressed when reading both the journal entries and informal writing the students do. The students should instead focus on expressing their thoughts and conveying their ideas. Conventional spelling and grammar will be stressed in formal writing assignments. However, the more students write, the more conventional spelling, grammar, and punctuation will be reflected in all of their writing.

Example:

Informal Writing

Informal writing in the four areas outlined below gives students many opportunities to express themselves creatively and to exercise writing as a life skill.

- Original Stories—original fiction the students invent
- Personal Experiences—relating incidents that have happened to them
- Expository Writing—writing about a specific subject, such as in a report
- Persuasive Writing—writing intended to convince the reader or influence his or her thinking

Examples of each kind of writing the students complete should be filed in the students' writing portfolios to illustrate growth.

Formal Writing

A formal writing experience in which a specific grammar or mechanics skill or concept is stressed should be offered to fluent learners at least once a week. During the week following the assignment, students can be asked to apply the learned concept in their journals and informal writing assignments. Formal writing assignments should be corrected only for the skill being taught, as students should come to fully understand one concept before moving on to a new one. However, because formal writing assignments are intended to be read by an audience, they should be free of grammatical, spelling, and punctuation errors. Students may achieve this by completing the editing process.

The Editing Process

The teacher should help students complete the editing process (prewriting, writing a first draft, revising, editing, and publishing) until it becomes second nature to them.

Prewriting
Gather ideas and information, then organize it.

First Draft
Write ideas on paper. Don't pay attention to spelling, punctuation, and grammar.

Revising
Reread story or have a partner read it aloud to you. Listen for areas that need additional work. Make any necessary changes.

Editing
Check and double-check your spelling, punctuation, and grammar. Correct for errors.

Publishing
Share your work with an audience.

ASSESSMENT OF THE WRITING PORTFOLIO USING THE INDIVIDUAL WRITING PROFILE

To facilitate the assessment of skills and concepts revealed in journal, informal, and formal writing assignments, an *Individual Writing Profile* form for each skill level has been developed: emergent learners (pages 60–61), developing learners (pages 62–63), and fluent learners (pages 64–65).

Each form is divided into four categories. The **Writing Experiences** section lists concepts students should practice on a daily basis. These activities reflect reading ability as well as writing ability. The section on **Sentences and Paragraphs** allows the teacher to chart growth as student writing matures and becomes more complex. The **Spelling** section highlights word attack skills and the correlation between hearing and writing sounds in emergent learners. In developing and fluent learners, teachers can track word attack skills and sight words. Teachers should observe a correlation between the improvement of spelling ability and writing ability. The final section tracks **Mechanics.** The mechanics of writing are taught in formal writing assignments and reinforced and reflected in daily writing assignments, such as journal and informal writing.

The *Individual Writing Profile* form has been designed to allow for teacher comments and for each assignment to be dated. Note that the form also allows for many different skills and concepts to be observed and assessed in one writing assignment entry.

Also included for each skill level (emergent, page 66; developing, page 67; fluent, page 68) is a *Whole Group Writing Profile* form designed to provide the teacher with an overall view of the class's progress. It contains the same categories as the *Individual Writing Profile* form.

How To Use the Individual Writing Profile

Make notations on the *Individual Writing Profile* of significant growth in a student's writing over the course of the year. The profile should reflect the overall progress the student has made. Every writing sample is not recorded.

There are two ways to manage the *Individual Writing Profile* :

- Make notations regularly every few weeks, or quarterly.
                              OR
- Make notations whenever individual pieces of writing demonstrate growth.

Example:

INDIVIDUAL WRITING PROFILE

SENTENCES / PARAGRAPHS	DATE			TEACHER COMMENTS
Scribble writes or string of letters				
Copies from the board	10/1			10/1 Added own sent. "i et tu"
Spaces words properly	11/6			
Completes sentence frame	9/6	11/1		
Copies a personal letter				
	10/1	11/3	12/6	
Writes 2 or more original sentences	2/5	4/19		4/19 Story - 2 pages!
Sentence patterns more complex	5/2			

Additional Comments: Andy' story-writing ability grew over the year.
He has wonderful imagination! He often writes on his own time.

File in the writing portfolio only the writing samples that are entered on the *Individual Writing Profile,* and keep the writing portfolios in an easily accessible spot. Frequent additions will be made to them, and students periodically may wish to read their own work.

Representative student papers showing an understanding of the concepts taught in math, science, and social studies should be placed in these portfolios.

MATH

Math skills are easy to assess. In each student's portfolio simply keep samples of student work that reflects an understanding of each math concept listed below. These concepts are based on the minimum competencies detailed in Chapter 3, pages 25–31. A *Math Continuum* form for recording assessments is included for each skill level (emergent learners, pages 69–70; developing learners, pages 71–72; fluent learners, pages 73–75).

NUMBERS/NUMERATION

Counting	Before/After, Greater	Place Value
Identifying/Writing	Than/Less Than	Even/Odd Numbers
Numbers	Sequencing	Prime Numbers
Matching Objects with	Ordinal Numbers	Roman Numerals
Numbers	<, >, =	
Classifying Objects	Count by 2s/5s/10s	

OPERATIONS

Addition	Fractions	Converting Fractions/
Subtraction	Decimals	Decimals/Percents
Multiplication	(including money)	
Division		

GEOMETRY

2- and 3-Dimensional	Equivalent Shapes	Coordinates (graphing)
Shapes	Congruence	Angles
Figures (parallel lines, etc.)	Circle Parts	
Symmetry	Perimeter/Area/Volume	

MEASUREMENT

Length	Time	(Fahrenheit/Celsius)
(inches/feet/yards,	Standard/Non-standard	Convert Standard Units
centimeter/meter)	Units	Capacity
Appropriate	Money	(pint/quart/gallon)
Measurements	Thermometer	

PROBLEM-SOLVING

Patterning	Number Sentences	Ratios and Probability
Word Problems	Equivalent Equations	Rounding
Estimating	Averages: Mean/Median	

INTERPRETATION

Tables/Charts/Graphs	Maps/Diagrams

SCIENCE AND SOCIAL STUDIES

Thematic units are the recommended method for structuring instruction in a whole language classroom. They make planning more manageable for teachers and learning easier for students. Thematic units are often based on science and social studies themes, and all of the reading, writing, and math the students do are related to that theme.

Examples of the reading, writing, and math activities based on science and social studies thematic units should be included in each student's science and social studies portfolio. (Note: Occasionally, a writing sample will be put in a student's writing portfolio if it shows growth in a particular area listed on the *Individual Writing Profile*.)

Listed below are appropriate thematic units in science and social studies for each grade and developmental learning level.

EMERGENT LEARNERS

	SCIENCE	*SOCIAL STUDIES*
Grade K:	My Body Health and Nutrition Seasons Five Senses Animals (farm, zoo, etc.) Community Helpers	All About Me (feelings, friends, self-esteem) My Family and Home Children Around the World Schools Community Helpers
Grade 1:	Sea Life Animals/Habitats Plants Dental Health Weather/Seasons	Where I Live/My Family Self-esteem Community Helpers Beginning Map Skills Native Americans Worldwide Celebrations

DEVELOPING LEARNERS

	SCIENCE	*SOCIAL STUDIES*
Grade 2:	Food Groups/Health Weather Plants Animals (habitats/adapting) Sea Life Environment/Ecology	Map Skills Multicultural Education African Americans Native Americans Asian Americans Community Helpers

DEVELOPING LEARNERS (continued)

	SCIENCE	*SOCIAL STUDIES*
Grade 3:	Insects Dinosaurs Solar System Ecology Rocks/Minerals Land/Sea Animals	Geography Map/Globe Skills Our Country Multicultural Education Native Americans/Pilgrims

FLUENT LEARNERS

	SCIENCE	*SOCIAL STUDIES*
Grade 4:	Flight/Machines Animal Kingdom (predator/prey) Magnets/Electricity Human Body Earthquakes/Volcanoes Ecology	State History Geography/Maps/Globes Feeling/Emotions My Family History Appreciating Other Cultures
Grade 5:	Plants and Animals Solar System (universe/rockets) Ecology Human Body Systems	American History North American Neighbors Map/Globe Skills
Grade 6:	Geology Environment/Ecology Our Body	Ancient Civilizations Geography/Maps World Cultures/Food/ Celebrations

NOTE: Many themes are repeated through the grades, but different concepts are taught in each level.

SHOWCASE PORTFOLIO

A Showcase Portfolio is a collection of work intended for public display and, therefore, should contain the best examples of a student's work across the curriculum. This portfolio can be shown at a Back-to-School Night or Open House as a display of a student's achievements. When compiling this portfolio, each student should be allowed to help choose work to be included.

CAUTION: The showcase portfolio should not be the only student work parents see. It can cause unrealistic expectations as real learning involves making mistakes.

Let students help choose their best work for the Showcase Portfolio.

The Showcase Portfolio is intended for public display.

Make sure parents see other samples of their child's work to better understand the whole learning process.

ANECDOTAL RECORDS

Teachers need a centralized place in which to store their records and anecdotal records on each student. No more than two collections of this work is necessary. The first will be a folder containing informal assessments and their notations (see Chapter 4, pages 37-44, for more information), and an audio tape recording of the student reading aloud. The other will be a three-ring binder that contains the *Individual Writing Profiles* and *Math Continuums* outlined in this chapter and the results of reading conferences (see Chapter 7, pages 83-110, for more details).

Informal assessments, reading records, conferences, and observations

Audio tape of student reading

Individual Writing Profiles, Whole Group Writing Profiles, and Math Continuums

STORAGE SECRETS

Portfolios need not take up an inordinate amount of space in the classroom. By using durable folders, inexpensive plastic crates, sturdy banker's boxes, or three-ring binders, all portfolios can be easily and securely stored.

Hanging files in a plastic crate can house portfolios.

A folded cardboard banker's box holds a small group's folders and audio tapes. The box fits in a filing cabinet.

Three-ring binders can hold anecdotal records, profiles, and continuums.

Manila folders stored in a cardboard storage box work well. Metal storage bins can also be used.

Accordion files hold portfolios for small groups. These files fit neatly in a filing cabinet.

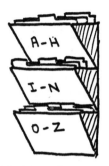

Plastic wall-mounted files make folders easily accessible.

No matter which storage method is used, make sure it fits comfortably into your classroom organizational pattern. Portfolios should not create more work, but make classroom assessment more manageable.

WHAT TO DO WITH THE PORTFOLIO AT THE END OF THE YEAR

Teachers and principals must come to some sort of consensus on how to house portfolios at the end of the school year. Individual teachers must also decide how much of each student's portfolio to pass on to the next year's teacher.

Typically between three and five writing samples, along with each *Individual Writing Profile,* are sufficient to illustrate to a new teacher what the student knows. The remainder of information in the portfolio can be sent home with the student.

EXAMPLES OF ACTUAL PORTFOLIOS

On the next page are examples of student work placed into the three types of portfolios outlined in this chapter: writing, math/science/social studies, and showcase.

Student Samples

WRITING PORTFOLIO
Samples of student writing, collected periodically

Daily Journal
- Reaction to literature and other reading

Informal Writing
- Original stories
- Poems
- Personal experiences
- Expository and persuasive writing

Formal Writing
- Rough drafts and finished pieces

MATH/SCIENCE/SOCIAL STUDIES PORTFOLIO
Samples of student work that show concepts the student has learned

Math Papers
- Samples illustrate understanding of math concepts

Science and Social Studies Assignments
- Samples show understanding of science and social studies themes

Informal Assessments
- Samples of appropriate informal assessments involving math/science/ social studies concepts (Depending on the filing method, informal assessments can be placed in either a student's folder or the teacher's folder.)

SHOWCASE PORTFOLIO
Examples of a student's best work

Major Classroom Projects
- Published stories
- Maps/charts/graphs
- Science experiments
- Art projects

Individual Writing Profile – EMERGENT LEARNERS (Grades K-1)

Student Name _____ Grade _____ School Year _____

WRITING EXPERIENCES	Date*					Teacher Comments
Journal Writing • • • • • • • • • • •						
Recalls Details						
Sequences Events						
Relates Story To Personal Experiences						
Draws Conclusions						
Predicts Outcomes						
Compares/Contrasts						
Real/Make-Believe						
Informal Writing • • • • • • • • • • •						
Original Stories........						
Personal Experiences						
Formal Writing • • • • • • • • • • •						
Applies Learned Concept........						
Additional Comments						

* May wish to record once each instructional quarter of the school year

CONTINUED – Individual Writing Profile – EMERGENT LEARNERS (Grades K-1)

Student Name _____ Grade _____ School Year _____

SENTENCES/PARAGRAPHS

Date* | | | | *Teacher Comments*

Scribble Writes/Writes Strings Of Letters ....
Copies From The Board ....
Spaces Words Properly...........
Completes Sentence Frame ....
Copies A Personal Letter ....
Writes Own Simple Sentence ....
Writes Two Or More Original Sentences...........
Sentence Patterns Are More Complex ....

Additional Comments

SPELLING

Date* | | | | *Teacher Comments*

Invented Spelling ••••••••••••
Writes Some Beginning Letters ....
Uses Correct Beginning/Ending Sounds ....
Uses Correct Beginning/Middle/Ending Sounds...
Conventional Spelling ••••••••••••
Some Commonly Used Words Spelled Correctly .

Additional Comments

MECHANICS

Date* | | | | *Teacher Comments*

Capitalization ••••••••••••••••
Capitalizes Beginning Of Sentence...........
Capitalizes "I" ....
Punctuation ••••••••••••
Punctuates End Of Sentence...........
Uses Question Mark ....
Grammar ••••••••••••
Uses Simple Subject/Verb Agreement ....

Additional Comments

* *May wish to record once each instructional quarter of the school year*

©1995 by Incentive Publications, Inc., Nashville, TN.

Individual Writing Profile – DEVELOPING LEARNERS (Grades 2–3)

Student Name _____   Grade _____   School Year _____

WRITING EXPERIENCES

Date*   Teacher Comments

Journal Writing •••••••••••••
- Recalls Details
- Sequences Events
- Relates Story To Personal Experiences
- Understands Main Idea
- Understands Cause/Effect Relationships
- Draws Conclusions
- Predicts Outcomes
- Compares/Contrasts
- Analyzes Character
- Real/Make-Believe
- Summarizes Plot

Informal Writing ••••••••••••••
- Original Stories
- Personal Experiences
- Expository Writing

Formal Writing •••••••••••••
- Applies Learned Concept
- Edits For Spelling, Punctuation, Grammar

Additional Comments

SENTENCES/PARAGRAPHS

Date*   Teacher Comments

- Sentence Patterns Are More Complex
- Writes Two Or More Original Sentences
- Writes To Topic
- Uses Vivid Words
- Writes Poetry
- Writes A Personal Letter
- Uses Paragraph Form
- Organizes Info. Into Paragraphs/Reports

Additional Comments

* May wish to record once each instructional quarter of the school year

©1995 by Incentive Publications, Inc., Nashville, TN.

Student Name _____ Grade _____ School Year _____

SPELLING

Date* Teacher Comments

Invented Spelling •••••••••••••••••

Uses Correct Beginning/Ending Letters............

Uses Correct Beginning/Middle/Ending Letters....

Conventional Spelling •••••••••••••

Spells Commonly Used Words Correctly.............

Spells Many Words Correctly.............

Uses Conventional Spelling Often................

Additional Comments

MECHANICS

Date* Teacher Comments

Capitalization •••••••••••••••

Capitalizes Beginning Of Sentence.............

Capitalizes "I" ....

Capitalizes Proper Nouns ....

Punctuation •••••••••••••••••

Punctuates End Of Sentence (? . !).............

Uses Commas In A Series................

Uses Apostrophes Correctly................

Grammar ••••••••••••••

Uses Simple Subject/Verb Agreement.............

Correct Word Usage................

Additional Comments

* May wish to record once each instructional quarter of the school year

©1995 by Incentive Publications, Inc., Nashville, TN.

Individual Writing Profile – FLUENT LEARNERS (Grades 4-6)

Student Name _____ Grade _____ School Year _____

WRITING EXPERIENCES

Date*   Teacher Comments

Journal Writing••••••••••••

Recalls Details/Sequences Events ....

Relates Story To Personal Experiences ....

Understands Main Idea ....

Understands Cause/Effect Relationships ....

Draws Conclusions ....

Predicts Outcomes ....

Compares/Contrasts ....

Analyzes Character/Setting ....

Summarizes Plot ....

Fact/Opinion ....

Mood ....

Understands Author's Tone/Intent ....

Informal Writing•••••••••••

Original Stories ....

Personal Experiences ....

Expository Writing ....

Persuasive Writing ....

Formal Writing •••••••••••••

Applies Learned Concept ....

Completes Editing Process (Prewriting/

1st Draft/Revising/Editing/Publishing) ....

Additional Comments

* May wish to record once each instructional quarter of the school year

CONTINUED – Individual Writing Profile – FLUENT LEARNERS (Grades 4-6)

Student Name _____ Grade _____ School Year _____

SENTENCES/PARAGRAPHS

Date* | | | | Teacher Comments

- Sentence Patterns Are More Complex..............
- Writes To Topic.............
- Writes Original Paragraphs ....
- Uses Vivid Words ....
- Writes Poetry ....
- Writes A Personal Letter ....
- Writes A Business Letter ....
- Organizes Info. Into Paragraphs/Reports............

Additional Comments

SPELLING

Date* | | | | Teacher Comments

Invented Spelling ••••••••••••••••••
- Approximates Spelling Of Unfamiliar Words ......

Conventional Spelling ••••••••••••••••
- Consistent Use Of Conventional Spelling ....
- Uses References To Spell Unfamiliar Words ....

Additional Comments

MECHANICS

Date* | | | | Teacher Comments

Capitalization ••••••••••••••••••••••••••
- Capitalizes Beginning Of Sentence/"I" ....
- Capitalizes Proper Nouns ....

Punctuation •••••••••••••••••••••••••
- Punctuates End Of Sentence (? . !) ....
- Uses Commas Correctly ....
- Uses Apostrophes Correctly.................
- Uses Quotation Marks Correctly.................
- Uses Colons Correctly ....

Grammar ••••••••••••••••••••••••
- Uses Complex Subject/Verb Agreement.............
- Correct Word Usage ....

Additional Comments

* May wish to record once each instructional quarter of the school year

©1995 by Incentive Publications, Inc., Nashville, TN.

Whole Group Writing Profile
Emergent (Grades K-1)

Teacher _____

Year _____

NAME

WRITING EXPERIENCES—JOURNAL/INFORMAL/FORMAL
- Recalls Details
- Sequences Events
- Relates Story To Personal Experiences
- Draws Conclusions
- Predicts Outcomes
- Compares/Contrasts
- Real/Make-Believe
- Original Stories
- Personal Experiences
- Applies Learned Concept

SENTENCES/PARAGRAPHS
- Scribble Writes/Writes Strings Of Letters
- Copies From The Board
- Spaces Words Properly
- Completes Sentence Frame
- Copies A Personal Letter
- Writes Own Simple Sentence
- Writes Two Or More Original Sentences
- Sentence Patterns Are More Complex

SPELLING—INVENTED/CONVENTIONAL
- Writes Some Beginning Letters
- Uses Correct Beginning/Ending Sounds
- Uses Correct Beginning/Middle/Ending Sounds
- Some Commonly Used Words Spelled Correctly

MECHANICS—CAPITALIZATION/PUNCTUATION/GRAMMAR
- Capitalizes Beginning Of Sentence
- Capitalizes "I"
- Punctuates End Of Sentence
- Uses Question Mark
- Uses Simple Subject/Verb Agreement

1.
2.
3.
4.
5.
6.
7.
8.
9.
10.
11.
12.
13.
14.
15.
16.
17.
18.
19.
20.
21.
22.
23.
24.
25.
26.
27.
28.
29.
30.

Whole Group Writing Profile
Developing (Grades 2-3)

Teacher _____

Year _____

NAME	WRITING EXPERIENCES—JOURNAL/INFORMAL/FORMAL														SENTENCES/PARAGRAPHS											SPELLING—INVENTED/CONVENTIONAL				MECHANICS—CAPITALIZATION/PUNCTUATION/GRAMMAR								
	Recalls Details	Sequences Events	Relates Story To Personal Experiences	Understands Main Idea	Understands Cause/Effect Relationships	Draws Conclusions	Predicts Outcomes	Compares/Contrasts	Analyzes Character	Real/Make-Believe	Summarizes Plot	Original Stories	Personal Experiences	Expository Writing	Applies Learned Concept	Edits For Spelling, Punctuation, Grammar	Sentence Patterns Are More Complex	Writes Two Or More Original Sentences	Writes To Topic	Uses Vivid Words	Writes Poetry	Writes A Personal Letter	Uses Paragraph Form	Organizes Info. Into Paragraphs/Reports	Uses Correct Beginning/Ending Letters	Uses Correct Beginning/Middle/Ending Letters	Spells Commonly Used Words Correctly	Spells Many Words Correctly	Uses Conventional Spelling Often	Capitalizes Beginning Of Sentence	Capitalizes "I"	Capitalizes Proper Nouns	Punctuates End Of Sentence (? . !)	Uses Commas In A Series	Uses Apostrophes Correctly	Uses Simple Subject/Verb Agreement	Correct Word Usage
1.																																					
2.																																					
3.																																					
4.																																					
5.																																					
6.																																					
7.																																					
8.																																					
9.																																					
10.																																					
11.																																					
12.																																					
13.																																					
14.																																					
15.																																					
16.																																					
17.																																					
18.																																					
19.																																					
20.																																					
21.																																					
22.																																					
23.																																					
24.																																					
25.																																					
26.																																					
27.																																					
28.																																					
29.																																					
30.																																					

Whole Group Writing Profile
Fluent (Grades 4-6)

Teacher _____

Year _____

NAME

1. 2. 3. 4. 5. 6. 7. 8. 9. 10. 11. 12. 13. 14. 15. 16. 17. 18. 19. 20. 21. 22. 23. 24. 25. 26. 27. 28. 29. 30.

WRITING EXPERIENCES—JOURNAL/INFORMAL/FORMAL

- Recalls Details/Sequences Events
- Relates Story To Personal Experiences
- Understands Main Idea
- Understands Cause/Effect Relationships
- Draws Conclusions
- Predicts Outcomes
- Compares/Contrasts
- Analyzes Character/Setting
- Summarizes Plot
- Fact/Opinion
- Mood
- Understands Author's Tone/Intent
- Original Stories
- Personal Experiences
- Expository Writing
- Persuasive Writing
- Applies Learned Concept
- Completes Editing Process (Prewriting/1st Draft/Revising/Editing/Publishing)

SENTENCES/PARAGRAPHS

- Sentence Patterns Are More Complex
- Writes To Topic
- Writes Original Paragraphs
- Uses Vivid Words
- Writes Poetry
- Writes A Personal Letter
- Writes A Business Letter
- Organizes Info. Into Paragraphs/Reports

SPELLING—INVENTED/CONVENTIONAL

- Approximates Spelling of Unfamiliar Words
- Consistent Use Of Conventional Spelling
- Uses References To Spell Unfamiliar Words

MECHANICS—CAPITALIZATION/PUNCTUATION/GRAMMAR

- Capitalizes Beginning Of Sentence/"I"
- Capitalizes Proper Nouns
- Punctuates End Of Sentence (? . !)
- Uses Commas Correctly
- Uses Apostrophes Correctly
- Uses Quotation Marks Correctly
- Uses Colons Correctly
- Uses Complex Subject/Verb Agreement
- Correct Word Usage

©1995 by Incentive Publications, Inc., Nashville, TN.

Math Continuum
KINDERGARTEN

Teacher _____

Year _____

NUMBERS/NUMERATION

- Counts To 10
- Counts To 20
- Identifies Numbers 1–10
- Identifies Numbers 1–20
- Writes Numbers To 10
- Writes Numbers To 20
- Matches Objects With Numbers 1–10
- Knows Before/After (To 10)
- Knows Greater/Less (To 10)
- Classifies Objects By 1 Attribute
- Classifies Objects By 2 Attributes

OPERATIONS

- Knows Addition Facts To 10

GEOMETRY

- Identifies Basic Geometric Shapes
- Draws Basic Geometric Shapes
- Understands Symmetry

MEASUREMENT

- Long/Longer/Longest
- Short/Shorter/Shortest
- Identifies Money (1¢, 5¢, 10¢, 25¢)

PROBLEM-SOLVING

- Completes Patterns Of Shapes

NAME

1.
2.
3.
4.
5.
6.
7.
8.
9.
10.
11.
12.
13.
14.
15.
16.
17.
18.
19.
20.
21.
22.
23.
24.
25.
26.
27.
28.
29.
30.

©1995 by Incentive Publications, Inc., Nashville, TN.

Math Continuum
FIRST GRADE

Teacher _____

Year _____

NAME

	Reads Maps	Reads Simple Graphs	INTERPRETATION	Solves Simple Word Problems (Orally)	Solves Number Sentences	Knows Simple Number Patterns	Completes Patterns Of Shapes	PROBLEM-SOLVING	Adds Money To 30¢	Identifies Money (1¢, 5¢, 10¢, 25¢, $1.00)	Reads Calendar	Tells Time To Half-Hour	Tells Time To Hour	Measures With Nonstandard Units	MEASUREMENT	Identifies Similar Shapes	Understands Symmetry	Draws Basic Shapes	GEOMETRY	Adds 2 Digits Without Regrouping	Adds 3 Numbers	Knows Addition Facts To 10	OPERATIONS	Knows Place Value (1s, 10s)	Identifies Ordinal Place (1st–10th)	Classifies Objects By 2 Attributes	Counts By 5s, 10s To 100	Sequences 3 Numbers (1–20)	Knows Greater/Less (To 100)	Knows Greater/Less (To 20)	Knows Before/After (To 100)	Knows Before/After (To 20)	Writes Numbers To 100	Writes Numbers To 20	NUMBERS/NUMERATION
1.																																			
2.																																			
3.																																			
4.																																			
5.																																			
6.																																			
7.																																			
8.																																			
9.																																			
10.																																			
11.																																			
12.																																			
13.																																			
14.																																			
15.																																			
16.																																			
17.																																			
18.																																			
19.																																			
20.																																			
21.																																			
22.																																			
23.																																			
24.																																			
25.																																			
26.																																			
27.																																			
28.																																			
29.																																			
30.																																			

Math Continuum
SECOND GRADE

Teacher _____

Year _____

NAME

	NUMBERS/NUMERATION											OPERATIONS						GEOMETRY						MEASUREMENT								PROBLEM-SOLVING						INTERPRETATION	
	Knows Before/After (To 100)	Knows Greater/Less (To 100)	Sequences 3 Numbers (1–20)	Sequences 3 Numbers (1–100)	Counts By 5s, 10s	Counts By 2s, 5s, 10s	Identifies Ordinal Place (1st–10th)	Knows Place Value (1s, 10s)	Knows Place Value (1s, 10s, 100s)	Adds 3 Numbers	Adds Without Regrouping	Adds With Regrouping	Subtracts Without Regrouping	Subtracts With Regrouping	Identifies Fractions (1/2, 1/3, 1/4)	Draws Basic Shapes	Recognizes 2-, 3-dimensional Shapes	Understands Symmetry	Identifies Equivalent Shapes	Measures In Inches	Measures With Nonstandard Units	Tells Time To Half-Hour And Quarter-Hour	Reads Calendar	Adds Money To 30¢	Adds Money To $1.00	Reads A Thermometer	Completes Patterns Of Shapes	Completes Number Patterns	Solves Number Sentences	Solves Word Problems	Solves Equivalent Equations	Reads Simple Graphs/Charts	Reads Maps
1.																																	
2.																																	
3.																																	
4.																																	
5.																																	
6.																																	
7.																																	
8.																																	
9.																																	
10.																																	
11.																																	
12.																																	
13.																																	
14.																																	
15.																																	
16.																																	
17.																																	
18.																																	
19.																																	
20.																																	
21.																																	
22.																																	
23.																																	
24.																																	
25.																																	
26.																																	
27.																																	
28.																																	
29.																																	
30.																																	

Math Continuum
THIRD GRADE

Teacher _____

Year _____

NAME

Columns numbered 1. through 30.

NUMBERS/NUMERATION
- Knows Place Value To 100s
- Knows Place Value To 1000s
- Understands Before/After, Greater/Less To 100
- Understands Before/After, Greater/Less To 1000
- Sequences Numbers To 1000
- Knows Ordinal Numbers To 10th
- Understands Even/Odd Numbers
- Knows <, >, =

OPERATIONS
- Adds With Regrouping
- Subtracts With Regrouping
- Multiplies Without Regrouping
- Multiplies With Regrouping
- Adds/Subtracts Money Problems
- Knows Multiplication facts To 5
- Knows Multiplication Facts To 9
- Knows Division Facts To 5
- Knows Division Facts To 9

GEOMETRY
- Knows Fractions: 1/8, 1/4, 1/3, 1/2
- Knows 2-, 3-dimensional Shapes
- Understands Symmetry
- Recognizes Equivalent Shapes/Congruence
- Knows Perimeter
- Knows Area

MEASUREMENT
- Measures In Inches: 1/2", 1/4"
- Measures In Centimeters
- Tells Time To Quarter-Hour
- Tells Time To 5 Minutes
- Reads A Calendar
- Knows Capacity (Pint/Quart/Gallon)
- Reads A Thermometer

PROBLEM-SOLVING
- Sees Number Patterns
- Solves Word Problems
- Writes Number Sentences
- Solves Equivalent Equations
- Estimates

INTERPRETATION
- Interprets Tables/Graphs/Charts
- Reads Maps

Math Continuum
FOURTH GRADE

Teacher _____

Year _____

NAME

	NUMBERS/NUMERATION								OPERATIONS							GEOMETRY							MEASUREMENT							PROBLEM-SOLVING					INTERPRETATION	
	Knows Place Value To 1000s	Understands Before/After, Greater/Less To 1000	Sequences Numbers To 1000	Knows Decimals To Tenths	Understands Even/Odd Numbers	Knows <, >, =	Knows Roman Numerals		Adds/Subtracts With Regrouping	Adds/Subtracts Money Problems	Adds/Subtracts Decimals	Multiplies With Regrouping	Knows Division Facts To 9	Knows Division With Remainder	Adds/Subtracts Simple Fractions	Knows Equivalent Fractions	Knows 2-, 3-dimensional Shapes	Identifies Figures	Understands Symmetry	Recognizes Congruence/Equivalent Shapes	Knows Perimeter/Area/Volume	Understands Coordinates (Graphing)	Measures Inches/Feet/Yards/Centimeters/Meters	Applies Appropriate Standards Of Measure	Tells Time To 5 Minutes	Tells Correct Time	Knows Calendar Conversions	Knows Capacity (Cup/Pint/Quart/Gallon)	Reads A Thermometer (Fahrenheit/Celsius)	Sees Number Patterns	Solves Word Problems (Incl. Money Problems)	Understands Number Sentences	Solves Equivalent Equations	Estimates	Interprets Tables/Graphs/Charts	Reads Maps/Diagrams
1.																																				
2.																																				
3.																																				
4.																																				
5.																																				
6.																																				
7.																																				
8.																																				
9.																																				
10.																																				
11.																																				
12.																																				
13.																																				
14.																																				
15.																																				
16.																																				
17.																																				
18.																																				
19.																																				
20.																																				
21.																																				
22.																																				
23.																																				
24.																																				
25.																																				
26.																																				
27.																																				
28.																																				
29.																																				
30.																																				

©1995 by Incentive Publications, Inc., Nashville, TN.

Math Continuum
FIFTH GRADE

Teacher _____

Year _____

NAME

NUMBERS/NUMERATION

- Sequences Numbers
- Understands Even/Odd Numbers
- Knows >, <, =
- Knows Roman Numerals
- Knows Place Value/Decimals

OPERATIONS

- Adds/Subtracts Decimals
- Multiplies/Divides Decimals
- Multiplies With Regrouping
- Knows Division With Remainders
- Adds/Subtracts Fractions
- Multiplies Fractions
- Converts Fractions To Decimals

GEOMETRY

- Identifies Figures
- Identifies Angles (Obtuse/Acute/Right)
- Knows 2-, 3-dimensional Shapes
- Measures Circle Parts (Radius/Diameter/Circumference)
- Understands Symmetry
- Recognizes Congruence/Equivalent Shapes
- Knows Perimeter/Area/Volume
- Understands Coordinates (Graphing)

MEASUREMENT

- Measures Inches/Feet/Yards/Centimeters/Meters
- Use Appropriate Standards Of Measure
- Knows Capacity (Cup/Pint/Quart/Gallon)
- Converts Standard Measuring Units
- Tells Time
- Uses A Calendar
- Reads A Thermometer (Fahrenheit/Celsius)

PROBLEM-SOLVING

- Sees Number Patterns
- Solves Word Problems/Number Sentences
- Solves Equivalent Equations
- Estimates

INTERPRETATION

- Interprets Tables/Graphs/Charts
- Reads Maps/Diagrams

1. 2. 3. 4. 5. 6. 7. 8. 9. 10. 11. 12. 13. 14. 15. 16. 17. 18. 19. 20. 21. 22. 23. 24. 25. 26. 27. 28. 29. 30.

©1995 by Incentive Publications, Inc., Nashville, TN.

Math Continuum
SIXTH GRADE

Teacher _____

Year _____

NAME	Sequences Numbers	Understands Prime Numbers	Understands Even/Odd Numbers	Knows <, >, =	Knows Roman Numerals	Knows Place Value/Decimals/Whole Numbers	Adds/Subtracts/Multiplies/Divides Decimals	Adds/Subtracts/Multiplies With Regrouping	Divides With Remainders	Adds/Subtracts/Multiplies Fractions	Divides Fractions	Converts Fractions To Decimals/Percent	Identifies Figures/Angles (Obtuse/Acute/Right)	Knows 2-, 3-dimensional Shapes	Measures Circle Parts (Radius/Diameter/Circumference)	Understands Symmetry	Recognizes Congruence/Equivalent Shapes	Knows Perimeter/Area/Volume	Understands Coordinates (Graphing)	Measures Inches/Feet/Yards/Centimeters/Meters	Use Appropriate Standards Of Measure	Knows Capacity (Cup/Pint/Quart/Gallon)	Converts Standard Measuring Units	Tells Time	Uses A Calendar	Reads A Thermometer (Fahrenheit/Celsius)	Sees Number Patterns	Solves Word Problems/Number Sentences	Solves Equivalent Equations	Estimates	Uses Averages (Mean/Medium)	Knows Concept Of Rounding	Interprets Tables/Graphs/Charts	Reads Maps/Diagrams
	NUMBERS/NUMERATION						OPERATIONS						GEOMETRY							MEASUREMENT							PROBLEM-SOLVING						INTERPRETATION	
1.																																		
2.																																		
3.																																		
4.																																		
5.																																		
6.																																		
7.																																		
8.																																		
9.																																		
10.																																		
11.																																		
12.																																		
13.																																		
14.																																		
15.																																		
16.																																		
17.																																		
18.																																		
19.																																		
20.																																		
21.																																		
22.																																		
23.																																		
24.																																		
25.																																		
26.																																		
27.																																		
28.																																		
29.																																		
30.																																		

Chapter Six

OBSERVATION AND NOTATION: "KID WATCHING"

Observation is an important aspect of whole language evaluation. Not only is it necessary to see students in the process of using the skills they are being taught, it is also enjoyable to watch students interact naturally and share the concepts they are learning. This means of evaluation gives the teacher a unique opportunity to see the whole language classroom in action. Besides offering insight into each student's development, it can reaffirm a teacher's faith in his or her students and in the whole language process altogether.

Taking a few minutes a day to observe students in action can be one of the most refreshing experiences a whole language teacher can have. The manner of observation should remain informal, but the purpose should be clear—a decision should be made whether individual students, small groups, or the entire class is to be observed. Once that has been established, the form the notation takes will vary.

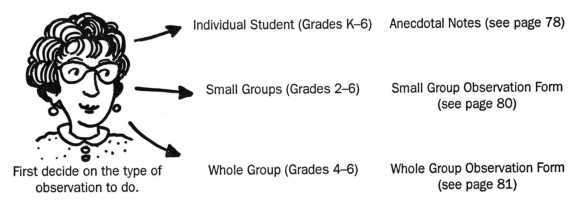

Types Of Notation

Individual Student (Grades K–6)   Anecdotal Notes (see page 78)

Small Groups (Grades 2–6)   Small Group Observation Form (see page 80)

First decide on the type of observation to do.

Whole Group (Grades 4–6)   Whole Group Observation Form (see page 81)

TYPES OF OBSERVATIONS

The type of notation will vary according to the type of observation the teacher will be doing. No matter which kind of observing the teacher does, however, time should be set aside in the daily schedule for the task. The most important aspects of observation are:

- Observe no more than once a day for five to fifteen minutes.
- Observe during different activities so that students can be seen in a variety of learning situations.

INDIVIDUAL STUDENT OBSERVATIONS

During a five- to fifteen-minute segment, the teacher observes a few students and makes anecdotal notes about each student. These notes can be made on 3" x 5" index cards, peel-off shipping labels, or on a page designated for each student in the teacher's anecdotal log.

3" x 5" index cards are dated and contain short observations.

Observations are dated and written on peel-off labels.

Labels are then stuck on pages designated for each student in an anecdotal log.
OR
Observations are written directly on the student's designated page in the log.

During these individual observations, the students should not realize they are being observed. After observing a student, the teacher then writes short anecdotal notes about what the student is doing or saying. After some time, an accurate profile of the student begins to emerge in a way no other form of evaluation could match.

Samples of individual student observations:

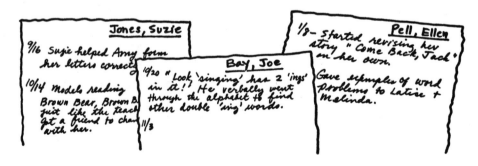

Emergent Learner
(Grades K–1)

Developing Learner
(Grades 2–3)

Fluent Learner
(Grades 4–6)

The teacher should try to observe two or three students a day during the observation time. This way, every student in the classroom will be observed approximately every four to six weeks.

SMALL GROUP OBSERVATION

Teachers should observe small groups to ascertain the students' time spent on-task and to make anecdotal notes about interaction skills. These anecdotal notes are less comprehensive than those for individual student observations.

Small group observations can be recorded on the *Small Group Observation Form* on page 80. It is a modified checklist with room for comments and other anecdotal remarks.

Example:

Small Group Observation Form

Date 4/19   Group Blue group

Names	On-Task	Task-Related	Off-Task	Comments/Anecdotes
			✓	Busy looking to others
1. Bay, Joe	✓			Takes leadership
2. Bell, L	✓			
3. Chen, R				
4.				
5.				

Small group observations should be made on developing and fluent learners only. Emergent learners have not developed the interpersonal skills necessary to successfully work in small groups. At best, emergent learners should begin to work in pairs.

WHOLE GROUP OBSERVATION

Observation of the whole class is usually done with fluent learners in the fourth through sixth grades. This is because the teacher is using a checklist of independent activities and projects only upper elementary grade students are capable of sustaining.

To assist the teacher with this type of observation, a *Whole Group Observation Form* is provided on page 81. It is a checklist adaptable to any class activity.

Example:

Whole Group Observation Form

Date 12/4   Activity History Report

Names	Reading	Uses Resources	Discuss Ideas	Info	Writing
1. Doe, J	X		X		X
2. Dahn, D		X			
3. Cable, H		X			
4. Jones, S			X	X	X

All teachers have been "kid watching" to one degree or another for years. Now, by organizing the observation process, "kid watching" can become a coherent and articulate assessment tool!

Small Group Observation Form

Date_____ Group_____

	Names	On-Task	Task-Related	Off-Task	Comments/Anecdotes
1.					
2.					
3.					
4.					
5.					
6.					
7.					
8.					
9.					
10.					
11.					
12.					

Date_____ Group_____

	Names	On-Task	Task-Related	Off-Task	Comments/Anecdotes
1.					
2.					
3.					
4.					
5.					
6.					
7.					
8.					
9.					
10.					
11.					
12.					

Whole Group Observation Form

Date_____ Activity _____

	Names	Reading	Uses Resources	Discuss Ideas	Info	Writing
1.						
2.						
3.						
4.						
5.						
6.						
7.						
8.						
9.						
10.						
11.						
12.						
13.						
14.						
15.						
16.						
17.						
18.						
19.						
20.						
21.						
22.						
23.						
24.						
25.						

Chapter Seven

READING RECORDS AND CONFERENCING

Maintaining reading records and conferencing with individual students are methods of evaluating reading skills, but they are not meant to be the foundation of a reading program. It is assumed that teachers will already be using a whole language approach to reading and will use these methods to assess it.

Depending on the level and abilities of the students, the teacher will want to assess different aspects of reading ability. These aspects fall into four general categories:
- Sight Vocabulary/Word Attack Skills
- Fluency
- Comprehension
- Personal Reading

By meeting with each individual student every four to six weeks, the teacher is able to assess the development of each aspect of reading ability. If used in conjunction with a wholistic approach to reading, conferencing can give teachers the traditional kind of reading information needed to assess growth.

It isn't necessary to review all aspects of reading in a conference; in fact, only one aspect should be observed during each conference.

SIGHT VOCABULARY/WORD ATTACK SKILLS

Word attack skills and the development of a sight vocabulary (words children immediately recognize "by sight" instead of sounding them out) are important skills for emergent and developing learners in grades 1–3. Fluent learners (grades 4–6) have already acquired a large sight vocabulary and, therefore, do not need to concentrate on this skill.

Just as there are steps to learning any new concept, there are steps to developing word attack skills and a sight vocabulary. First, emergent learners (K–1) learn the names and sounds of alphabet letters, then recognize them at the beginning, middle, and ending of words. Next, emergent learners are able to put together the sounds and decode them, then recognize simple phonetic words.

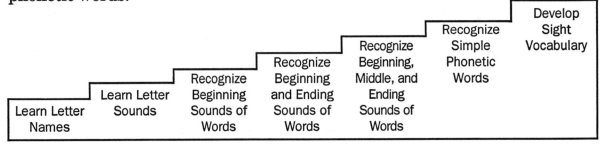

The wholistic literature-based approach introduces whole words and phrases to help children develop a sight vocabulary. This can be implemented in the classroom by having literature read aloud in class, charting stories, reading in pairs, reading silently, and listening to taped stories at a Listening Post.

Both approaches are taught and used simultaneously. When beginning to read, children need to have every means at their disposal to approximate the pronunciation of a word—phonetically and by sight.

One way to assess a child's sight vocabulary and subsequent word attack skills is through a list of high frequency words. High frequency words are those most commonly used by children in their natural speech and most often encountered in children's literature. Lists of high frequency words are provided on pages 99–102. They are listed in approximate order of difficulty.

High Frequency Words
The most commonly used words in children's natural speech and literature

Evaluation with Word Lists
The teacher marks sight words the child knows on appropriate words lists and notates word attack skills, if any.
(Note: Word lists are not good teaching tools. They should be used for evaluation purposes only.)

For the purposes of this book, acquiring word attack skills and a sight vocabulary are intended for emergent learners in grade 1 and developing learners in grades 2 and 3. It is important to stress that word lists taken out of context are not recommended teaching tools. They should be used for evaluation purposes only.

NOTATING WORD LISTS

Each word list is designated for either emergent (grade 1) or developing (grades 2–3) learners, and assigned an approximate reading level: beginning, early, average, or advanced. Before using any list, it is recommended that teachers review the words on the list, and add or subtract words as necessary.

To notate a word list, the teacher marks "S" for a sight word and "S/O" for a word the student has sounded out. If a student mispronounces a word, then corrects him- or herself and gives the right word, the teacher will write "SC" for self-correct. Words the student did not correctly identify should be circled, and the word given instead (if any) should be written on the paper.

The most these lists are designed to do is reveal the sight vocabulary a student has developed. If a student doesn't know a word by sight but can sound it out correctly, it is certain that word will soon become a sight word and will be readily recognized.

```
┌─────────────────────────────────────────────────────┐
│              Readability Chart                      │
│                                                     │
│  95% accuracy (3 mistakes)..............Go on to next list.   │
│                                                     │
│  90% accuracy (5 or 6 mistakes)......Stay put. Child is at   │
│                                     instructional level.     │
│                                                     │
│  Below 90% (6 or 7+ mistakes)........Move to an easier list. │
│                                     Child is at frustration  │
│                                     level.                   │
└─────────────────────────────────────────────────────┘
```

The Readability Chart is based on Marie Clay's contention that a student reading with 95 percent accuracy is reading easily and is ready for the next level of instruction. Reading with 90 percent accuracy is the perfect instructional level; anything less is too difficult. These same readability levels can be applied to reading fluency.

For years educators have used short passages from literature books to ascertain a student's reading fluency as well as sight vocabulary and basic comprehension. This approach is a good method of gaining an understanding of a student's overall reading ability.

Fluency has to do with a student's confidence and experience with reading. The better the words are known, the smoother the student's reading and comprehension are. However, when the student is not yet fluent, reading is done one word at a time in a halting manner. This allows for little comprehension.

The *Fluency Indicator* form on page 103 allows teachers to insert any 80–120 word passage and check a student's fluency—whether an emergent, developing, or fluent learner.

To choose a passage, teachers simply locate an interesting paragraph or paragraphs from an appropriate literature book. Preferably, the passage should come to some conclusion and not cut off at mid-sentence. Eighty to 120 words is a general count—going over a few words is of no consequence. To save time, the passage can be photocopied and taped onto a master copy of the *Fluency Indicator* form, and then duplicated.

Choose 80–120 word passage from an appropriate literature book.

Copy the passage and tape it to a master of the *Fluency Indicator.*

Student reads the actual book while the teacher notates the *Fluency Indicator* form.

APPROPRIATE LITERATURE BOOKS FOR FLUENCY

Below is a short list of appropriate books from which to excerpt passages for the fluency assessment.

Emergent Learners (Grades K–1)

The Cat in the Hat by Dr. Seuss
The Carrot Seed by Ruth Krauss
Too Many Books by Caroline Bauer
Are You My Mother? by P.D. Eastman
Danny and the Dinosaur by Syd Hoff
Frog and Toad Are Friends by Arnold Lobel
Caps for Sale by Esphyr Slobodkina
Chicken Soup With Rice by Maurice Sendak
If You Give a Mouse a Cookie by Laura Numeroff

Developing Learners (Grades 2–3)

Bunnicula by Deborah and James Howe
Hill of Fire by Thomas P. Lewis
James and the Giant Peach by Roald Dahl
Frog and Toad Together by Arnold Lobel
Freckle Juice by Judy Blume
The Drinking Gourd by F. M. Monjo
Fables by Arnold Lobel
The Courage of Sarah Noble by Alice Dalgliesh
The Mouse and the Motorcycle by Beverly Cleary
Sarah, Plain and Tall by Patricia MacLachlan

Fluent Learners (Grades 4–6)

Danny, the Champion of the World by Roald Dahl
My Side of the Mountain by Jean George
Hatchet by Gary Paulsen
Stone Fox by John R. Gardiner
Call It Courage by Armstrong Sperry
The Enormous Egg by Oliver Butterworth
The Railway Children by Edith Nesbit
Zia by Scott O'Dell
Dear Mr. Henshaw by Beverly Cleary
Paddle-to-the-Sea by Holling C. Holling

These are only suggestions. Any literature book appropriate to a grade or developmental level can be effectively used.

The sample *Fluency Indicator* below can be applied to any student who is a reader in grades K–6. The only difference, of course, will be the reading level of the passage chosen.

Fluency Indicator

Name **Suzie Jones** _____ Grade **3** Date **4/16**

Results	Recommendations
95% or above = Effortless	Go to next level
90% = Comfortable	Keep at present level
89% or below = Difficult	Go back a level

Notations (count each as an error)
SC = self corrects
⬭ = wrong word
actual word
⬭ = write the actual word child says

(insert 80-120 word passage)

"What a great idea!" said Victor. "I'll make a meal out of all my favorite foods."

First he got out some bread. Then he went through his house to gather all his favorite things to eat. He piled them on top of one another—cheese, jelly, popcorn and peanut butter. When he found more, he added to the pile he carefully balanced in his arms—fish, three hot dogs, one ham and a slice of cake.

Soon the pile of food was so high, he couldn't see where he was going. Crash! It fell into a heap and he ate it off the floor.

3 self corrections

4 misread words

7 mistakes total

Total = 104 words

Score		Fluency		
		Check One		Check One
A. Total # words	104	☐ Single Words		☐ Ignores Punctuation
B. # errors	7	☐ Erratic		☒ Observes Punctuation
C. Subtract B from A	97 ÷ 104	☒ Phrases		**Score** (Check One)
D. Divide C by A	93 %	☐ Natural		◯ 95% and Above = Effortless
		☐ Too Fast		⊗ 90–94% = Comfortable
				◯ 89% and Below = Difficult

103

After establishing a student's reading fluency, as shown in the example above, the teacher may wish to ask some comprehension questions about the passage.

The skills of comprehension and fluency are linked. The student who only reads one word at a time isn't comprehending much since all energy is going into word identification. The student who reads at a natural rate and self-corrects or inserts appropriate words is comprehending while reading. However, while reading fluency is assessed by reading aloud, comprehension is best assessed by silent reading.

When reading aloud, a child concentrates on correct pronunciation, sight words, and word attack skills. Even when that child's fluency is excellent, the level of comprehension exhibited through the use of context clues is far below the higher levels of comprehension. To adequately practice the literal, inferential, and critical thinking aspects of comprehension, children should become familiar with the text through silent reading.

Fluency is assessed by the student reading aloud while the teacher notates on the *Fluency Indicator.*

Comprehension is assessed by the student reading silently and then answering questions posed by the teacher. The teacher notates the student's responses on the *Reading Comprehension and Personal Reading Record.*

LEVELS OF COMPREHENSION

There are three basic levels of comprehension: literal, inferential, and critical thinking. The specific skills involved in each level, along with the appropriate grade levels at which each skill should be mastered, are listed on the *Scope and Sequence Chart of Whole Language Skills* on pages 13–14.

It is important to note that literal comprehension is the lowest level of comprehension, but it is used whenever inferential and critical thinking skills are employed. Therefore, literal comprehension is best stressed with emergent learners in grades K–1 to teach the concept, then used as a springboard to the inferential level. The same steps are followed for developing learners, but more emphasis should be placed on the inferential and critical thinking aspects of comprehension. Fluent learners are best directed exclusively to the inferential and critical thinking levels of comprehension since they utilize the literal aspect of comprehension when employing each skill.

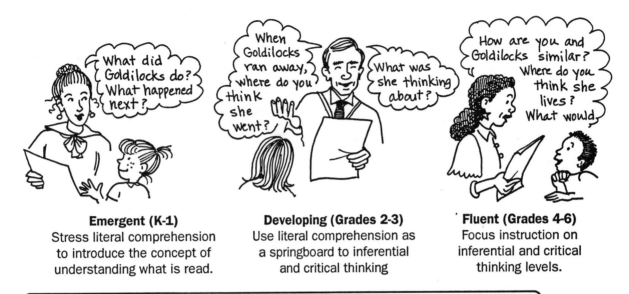

Emergent (K-1)
Stress literal comprehension to introduce the concept of understanding what is read.

Developing (Grades 2-3)
Use literal comprehension as a springboard to inferential and critical thinking

Fluent (Grades 4-6)
Focus instruction on inferential and critical thinking levels.

READING COMPREHENSION AND PERSONAL READING RECORD

The *Reading Comprehension and Personal Reading Record* allows the teacher to conference with each student and note growth in appropriate areas of comprehension. As the *Individual Writing Profile* assesses certain areas of reading comprehension through writing, this form allows the teacher to do the same by verbally questioning the student. Using both forms reveals the depth of a student's understanding.

Ways Children **Receive** Information

Hear it!

Read it!

Ways Children **Express** Information

Speak it!

Write it!

Reading Conferences

Writing Profiles

The *Reading Comprehension and Personal Reading Record* has been developed in two parts: reading comprehension and personal reading. The Reading Comprehension section reflects all skills and aspects of reading comprehension (literal, inferential, and critical thinking) and is tailored to meet the individual needs of each skill level. The Personal Reading section has been designed to allow teachers a place on which to record results of observations and discussion with a student about his or her personal reading habits and choices.

All conferences should be dated. Four boxes are provided for each aspect of comprehension so that the teacher may record a student's progress each instructional quarter of the school year. Forms are found on page 104 (emergent learner), page 106 (developing learner), and page 108 (fluent learner).

READING COMPREHENSION AND PERSONAL READING CLASS PROFILE

A class profile form to assess reading comprehension and personal reading habits has also been developed for each skill level (emergent learners, page 105; developing learners, page 107; fluent learners, page 109). It was designed to give a teacher a comprehensive view of the progress of an entire class.

COMPREHENSION QUESTIONS AND NOTATIONS

Sample questions for each level of comprehension are provided on pages 91–97, along with ways to notate reading records for emergent, developing, and fluent learners.

It must be stated that emergent learners in grades K–1 will have only listened to a story and not read it since beginning reading skills are still being taught. If, however, a teacher finds that he or she has a precocious child at this level, the child may read the story and respond accordingly to the questions. The teacher should then note that the emergent child has read the story. The teacher may instead choose to complete a developing learner's reading record for that student.

Otherwise, it is assumed that children at the developing (grades 2–3) and fluent (grades 4–6) levels will have read the story, passage, or chapter. Teachers should always have a copy of the book or passage available to which the student may refer during the conference.

LITERAL COMPREHENSION QUESTIONS

Note: Choose only one or two questions from each area.

Details
- Who did _____?
- What did the character do?
- Where did the story take place?
- Why did the character _____?
- When did the character _____?
- How did the character _____?

Pronoun Reference
- Who does the word "he" refer to in this story/sentence?
- If I said, "Why did 'he' do _____?", whom would I be talking about? (Replace the word "he" with any other pronoun—she, it, they, etc.)

Sequence
- What happened first in the story?
- What did the character do after _____?
- What did the character do before _____?
- What is the last thing that happened in the story?

Examples:

EMERGENT LEARNERS—Story: *The Three Bears*
Details
- What did Goldilocks do?
- What did Mama Bear say?
- What happened to Baby Bear's chair?

Pronoun Reference
- Whom am I talking about if I say, "She ate the bear's porridge?"

Sequence
- What was the last thing that happened in the story?
- What happened after the bears went for a walk?
- What did Goldilocks do before she tasted Papa Bear's porridge?

DEVELOPING LEARNERS—Story: *The Giving Tree*
Details
- What happened to the tree's apples?
- Why did the boy take the tree's branches?
- When was the tree lonely?

Pronoun Reference
- To what does "it" refer in the story?
- To whom does "he" refer in the story?

Sequence
- What was the first thing that happened in the story?
- What happened to the tree after it lost its branches?

FLUENT LEARNERS—Story: *James and the Giant Peach*
Details
- How did James end up living with his aunts?
- What happened to the magic green things?

Pronoun Reference
- To whom does "he" refer in the story?
- Name some of the "she's" in the story?

Sequence
- What happened before the giant peach grew?
- When did James meet the centipede?
- What happened after they landed in New York?

INFERENTIAL COMPREHENSION QUESTIONS

Note: Choose only one question from each area. All skills may not apply to every text. Use only those questions that lend themselves to the reading.

Relate Story to Personal Experiences
- Have you ever had something like this happen to you?
- Have you ever felt like the character? Tell about it.
- When have you had a similar experience?

Main Idea
- What different title would you give this story/passage/chapter? Explain why.
- Tell me what the story/passage/chapter is mostly about.
- What is the main idea?

Cause/Effect
- What made (caused) the character act the way he/she did?
- If _____ hadn't happened, would the character have done the same thing? Why?
- What effect did _____ have on the character?

Draw Conclusions
- Would the character make a good friend? Why?
- What can you tell me about this character?
- What do you think the character should do? Why?

Predict Outcomes
- What will happen next?
- How do you think the story will end?
- Make up another ending to the story/passage/chapter.

Compare/Contrast
- How are you and the character the same? Different?
- How are the two characters similar and different?

Examples:

EMERGENT LEARNERS—Story: *Ira Sleeps Over*

Relate Story to Personal Experiences
- Have you ever been afraid to spend the night with a friend? Tell about it.
- When have you felt like Ira?

Main Idea
- Tell me what the story was about.
- What could be another name for this story?

Cause/Effect
- What made Ira worry about spending the night with his friend?
- What was Ira's sister's attitude? How did he feel as a result?

Draw Conclusions
- What else could Ira have done to solve his problem?
- What can you tell about Ira from the story?

Predict Outcomes
- What would have happened if Ira hadn't brought his teddy bear?
- What would have happened if Reggie had laughed at Ira's teddy bear?

Compare/Contrast
- How was Ira the same as his friend Reggie?
- How are you and Ira different?
- How is Ira's teddy bear like your favorite toy?

DEVELOPING LEARNERS—Story: *Alexander and the Terrible, Horrible, No Good, Very Bad Day*

Relate Story to Personal Experiences
- Tell about a time you felt like Alexander.
- What makes a terrible, horrible day for you?

Main Idea
- What is the story mostly about?
- What could be another title for this story? Explain why.

Cause/Effect
- What made Alexander feel his cat didn't like him?
- If Alexander had found a prize in his cereal, how would he have felt?

Draw Conclusions
- What could be done to make Alexander feel better?
- What can you tell about Alexander?

Predict Outcomes
- How would Alexander's entire day have been different if it had started out differently?
- What will happen tomorrow for Alexander?

Compare/Contrast
- How is Alexander's bad day similar to and different from yours?
- How are his new shoes similar to his brother's shoes?

FLUENT LEARNERS—Story: *In the Year of the Boar and Jackie Robinson*

Relate Story to Personal Experiences
- Tell about an experience you had that was similar to Shirley's.
- Tell how you would feel if you had to move far away from your home.

Main Idea
- What other title would you give this chapter or book? Explain why.

- What is the chapter about?

Cause/Effect
- What things made Shirley afraid?
- How did Shirley deal with new situations and experiences?

Draw Conclusions
- Will Shirley be a good older sister? Explain why.
- Will Shirley get involved in another class election? Why?

Predict Outcomes
- What do you think Shirley will do in the next chapter? Why?
- Will Shirley keep following baseball? Why?

Compare/Contrast
- How is your favorite game the same as and different from baseball?
- How are China and the United States similar and different?

CRITICAL THINKING QUESTIONS

Note: Choose only one question from each area. All skills may not apply to every text. Use only those questions that lend themselves to the reading.

Analyze Character/Setting
- What can you tell me about the character/setting?
- What kinds of things do you think the character likes to do? Why?
- How is the setting important to the story?
- How would the story be different if the character/setting were different?

Real/Make-Believe
- Was _____ real or make-believe?
- Tell me something real/make-believe from the story.
- Could _____ really happen? Why?

Summarize
- Retell the story.
- What happened in the beginning/middle/end of the story?
- Tell me what the story/passage/chapter was about.
- Tell the story from a character's point of view.

Fact/Opinion
- Give an example of a fact/opinion from the story.
- Read this statement. Is it fact or opinion? How do you know?
- Do you agree with that statement? Why?

Mood
- What feeling does the story/passage/chapter give you? Why?
- Read this paragraph and tell me about the mood it sets.
- Retell the story using the mood it established.
- How does the setting of the story help set a mood?

Author's Tone/Intent
- What is the author trying to do by writing this?
- Why did the author write it?
- How is the author saying this?
- What feelings do you get from how the author wrote this piece?
- Pretend you are the author and explain why you wrote this.

Examples:

EMERGENT LEARNERS—Story: *If You Give a Mouse a Cookie*
Analyze Character
- Will the mouse keep taking cookies? Why?
- Would you want the mouse to be your friend? Why or why not?

Real/Make-Believe
- What was real in the story? What was make-believe?
- What could not happen in real life?

DEVELOPING LEARNERS—Story: *Knots on a Counting Rope*
Analyze Character
- How does the boy deal with his blindness?
- How would he be different if he could see?

Real/Make-Believe
- What is real about the story?
- Is there anything make-believe in the story? Explain.

Summarize
- Retell the story.
- Tell what the boy remembers in the story.

FLUENT LEARNERS—Story: *Sarah, Plain and Tall*
Analyze Character/Setting
- How is Sarah like the seashore?
- How would the story be different if it took place at the ocean?
- Will Sarah tire of the prairie?

Summarize
- Retell the story from Sarah's point of view.
- Tell the three main events in this chapter.

Fact/Opinion
- List facts and opinions about the seashore mentioned in this chapter.

Mood
- When Sarah describes the sea, how does it make you feel?
- What feelings do the last two paragraphs give you? Why?

Author's Tone/Intent
- Why does the author make us think Sarah might not come back?

Personal reading is the reading students do on their own. A teacher can learn a great deal about students' reading habits by noting the types of books they choose to read on their own. The teacher ascertains this information by observing each student and discussing their choices during reading conference time.

Observation
Teacher observes the student
at different times during the day.

Discussion
Teacher discusses with student
during reading conference time.

Information from both methods is notated on each child's *Reading Comprehension and Personal Reading Record*. Listed below are attributes to look for, questions to ask, and methods of notating teacher observations. Since the personal reading information is consistent throughout the grade levels, only one example is shown.

OBSERVATION (ATTRIBUTES TO LOOK FOR)

Note: Only one attribute needs to be exhibited.

Chooses To Read
- When schoolwork is finished, student chooses to read a book.
- Student reads at times when it is not required.
- Student asks to take class books home to read.

Selects Appropriate Books (can be observed during silent reading)
- Student chooses books appropriate to grade level and learning level.
- Student can read text or pictures.
- Student gravitates towards familiar books.

DISCUSSION (QUESTIONS TO ASK)

Note: Ask one or two questions, then look for one or two attributes to be exhibited.

Aware of Author/Illustrator
- "Who wrote/illustrated this book?"
- "Who is your favorite author/illustrator?"
- "Why?"
- "What do you like about this author's/illustrator's books?"

Selects Books by Subject (Attributes and Questions)

- Student uses card catalogue.
- Student knows where books on specific subjects are located.
- Student chooses appropriate books for reports.
- Student checks title, table of contents, or index.
- "What subjects do you like to read about?"
- "How many books have you read on that subject?"
- "Can you use the index to find information? Show me."

HOW TO MANAGE READING RECORDS AND CONFERENCES IN THE CLASSROOM

Fitting reading conferences into the daily schedule is not as difficult as it may seem. (It is assumed that teachers will be organizing reading groups on a daily basis.) After reading groups have met and students are involved in paired reading or seatwork activities, the teacher can take ten or fifteen minutes for conferences each day. In that amount of time, one to three students can be met with and evaluated. Using this method, each student will have a conference approximately every four to six weeks.

Schedule 10–15 minutes of conferencing or observation time per day. Each student will cycle through once every 4–6 weeks.

Call students for conferences after reading groups are finished.

Deal with one section of the *Reading Record* at a time so that the student and teacher are not overloaded with information.

Schedule observations for different times during the day. Five or 10 minutes before or after a transition, during silent reading, or during a whole group project are good times for the observations.

Name _____

HIGH FREQUENCY WORDS—EMERGENT LEARNERS (Grades K–1)

Beginning Reader Grade 1—List 1		**Early Reader** Grade 1—List 2	
Grade____ Date_____ %___		Grade____ Date_____ %___	
(5 mistakes = 90%)		*(5 mistakes = 90%)*	
1. I	26. big	1. you	26. they
2. can	27. did	2. with	27. to
3. and	28. find	3. just	28. good
4. see	29. for	4. made	29. have
5. go	30. all	5. down	30. much
6. do	31. sit	6. back	31. new
7. get	32. that	7. who	32. your
8. has	33. hand	8. call	33. or
9. on	34. has	9. long	34. away
10. now	35. he	10. may	35. best
11. no	36. her	11. was	36. does
12. me	37. him	12. way	37. give
13. make	38. my	13. what	38. here
14. it	39. not	14. when	39. last
15. is	40. of	15. from	40. old
16. in	41. sun	16. out	41. need
17. so	42. but	17. over	42. take
18. she	43. tell	18. said	43. us
19. the	44. got	19. some	44. went
20. we	45. let	20. then	45. put
21. will	46. cut	21. as	46. name
22. this	47. red	22. be	47. thing
23. look	48. at	23. by	48. men
24. man	49. his	24. same	49. like
25. up	50. just	25. its	50. saw

Name _____

HIGH FREQUENCY WORDS—EMERGENT LEARNERS (Grades K–1)

Average Reader
Grade 1—List 3

Grade____ Date_____ %___

(6 mistakes = 90%)

1. after	21. them	41. told
2. also	22. there	42. took
3. any	23. these	43. upon
4. are	24. time	44. want
5. been	25. too	45. play
6. your	26. two	46. feet
7. which	27. how	47. kind
8. about	28. most	48. land
9. little	29. one	49. say
10. many	30. where	50. seen
11. more	31. words	51. such
12. very	32. keep	52. can't
13. were	33. live	53. don't
14. other	34. above	54. began
15. than	35. but	55. show
16. back	36. almost	56. line
17. day	37. hard	57. didn't
18. called	38. help	58. being
19. if	39. move	59. better
20. into	40. must	60. end

Advanced Reader
Grade 1—List 4

Grade____ Date_____ %___

(6 mistakes = 90%)

1. around	21. mother	41. I'm
2. could	22. without	42. asked
3. first	23. toward	43. well
4. would	24. because	44. room
5. write	25. place	45. top
6. use	26. few	46. work
7. water	27. five	47. never
8. each	28. body	48. father
9. only	29. knew	49. while
10. our	30. large	50. why
11. people	31. school	51. those
12. right	32. sound	52. ever
13. their	33. still	53. try
14. know	34. often	54. turn
15. think	35. later	55. under
16. through	36. done	56. come
17. across	37. set	57. side
18. again	38. should	58. part
19. always	39. himself	59. going
20. another	40. home	60. below

Number Words

1. two	6. one
2. five	7. six
3. eight	8. nine
4. ten	9. three
5. four	10. seven

Color Words

1. blue	5. orange
2. black	6. red
3. yellow	7. green
4. brown	8. purple

Name _____

HIGH FREQUENCY WORDS—DEVELOPING LEARNERS (Grades 2-3)

Average Reader
Grade 2—List 5

Grade_____ Date_____ %___

(6 mistakes = 90%)

1. around	21. mother	41. I'm
2. could	22. top	42. asked
3. first	23. toward	43. because
4. would	24. well	44. room
5. write	25. place	45. without
6. use	26. few	46. work
7. water	27. five	47. never
8. each	28. body	48. father
9. only	29. knew	49. while
10. our	30. large	50. why
11. people	31. school	51. those
12. right	32. sound	52. ever
13. their	33. still	53. try
14. know	34. often	54. turn
15. think	35. later	55. under
16. through	36. done	56. come
17. across	37. set	57. side
18. again	38. should	58. part
19. always	39. himself	59. going
20. another	40. home	60. below

Advanced Reader
Grade 2—List 6

Grade_____ Date_____ %___

(6 mistakes = 90%)

1. against	21. today	41. blue
2. animal	22. every	42. girl
3. head	23. until	43. follow
4. money	24. car	44. everything
5. usually	25. small	45. cold
6. plants	26. paper	46. gone
7. fish	27. found	47. happy
8. both	28. between	48. person
9. sea	29. sure	49. horse
10. night	30. along	50. really
11. learn	31. end	51. inside
12. door	32. am	52. lost
13. great	33. ball	53. short
14. light	34. became	54. longer
15. house	35. yes	55. mind
16. read	36. walked	56. ready
17. near	37. tall	57. real
18. next	38. stop	58. six
19. far	39. before	59. seem
20. white	40. black	60. round

Number Words

1. two	11. eleven
2. five	12. fourteen
3. eight	13. seventeen
4. ten	14. fifteen
5. four	15. twelve
6. one	16. twenty
7. six	17. eighteen
8. nine	18. sixteen
9. three	19. thirteen
10. seven	20. nineteen

Color Words

1. blue
2. black
3. yellow
4. brown
5. orange
6. red
7. green

Ordinal Numbers

1. second
2. fifth
3. seventh
4. first
5. sixth
6. ninth
7. eighth
8. third
9. tenth
10. fourth

Name _____

HIGH FREQUENCY WORDS—DEVELOPING LEARNERS (Grades 2-3)

Average Reader
Grade 3—List 7

Grade_____ Date_____ %___

(6 mistakes = 90%)

1. air	21. thought	41. class
2. answer	22. together	42. start
3. hear	23. even	43. behind
4. true	24. change	44. boat
5. picture	25. since	45. caught
6. food	26. something	46. close
7. boy	27. once	47. ground
8. second	28. form	48. green
9. story	29. already	49. gave
10. off	30. ask	50. front
11. left	31. become	51. kept
12. during	32. yet	52. leave
13. group	33. wide	53. mean
14. might	34. watch	54. matter
15. high	35. third	55. nothing
16. country	36. ten	56. road
17. world	37. talk	57. shall
18. face	38. bring	58. shown
19. family	39. strong	59. buy
20. whole	40. remember	60. sky

Advanced Reader
Grade 3—List 8

Grade_____ Date_____ %___

(6 mistakes = 90%)

1. heard	21. children	41. bottom
2. morning	22. city	42. circle
3. point	23. soon	43. finally
4. came	24. own	44. either
5. study	25. page	45. stay
6. number	26. four	46. behind
7. life	27. beautiful	47. carefully
8. earth	28. yourself	48. grow
9. half	29. wrote	49. game
10. sentence	30. within	50. explain
11. several	31. whose	51. deep
12. different	32. whether	52. friend
13. however	33. though	53. color
14. important	34. it's	54. year
15. themselves	35. three	55. follow
16. happened	36. book	56. instead
17. mountain	37. brought	57. listen
18. example	38. certain	58. young
19. suddenly	39. teacher	59. music
20. enough	40. straight	60. yarn

Number Words

1. two	11. eleven
2. five	12. fourteen
3. eight	13. seventeen
4. ten	14. fifteen
5. four	15. twelve
6. one	16. twenty
7. six	17. eighteen
8. nine	18. sixteen
9. three	19. thirteen
10. seven	20. nineteen

Color Words

1. blue
2. black
3. yellow
4. brown
5. orange
6. red
7. green
8. purple

Ordinal Numbers

1. second
2. fifth
3. seventh
4. first
5. sixth
6. ninth
7. eighth
8. third
9. tenth
10. fourth

Fluency Indicator

Name _____ Grade _____ Date _____

Results	Recommendations
95% or above = Effortless............... Go to next level
90% = Comfortable............... Keep at present level
89% or below = Difficult................. Go back a level

Notations (count each as an error)
SC = self corrects
⬭ = wrong word
actual word
⬭ = write the actual word child says

(insert 80-120 word passage)

Score	**Fluency**	
	Check One	Check One
A. Total # words	☐ Single Words	☐ Ignores Punctuation
B. # errors	☐ Erratic	☐ Observes Punctuation
C. Subtract B from A	☐ Phrases	**Score** (Check One)
D. Divide C by A ___ %	☐ Natural	◯ 95% and Above = Effortless
	☐ Too Fast	◯ 90–94% = Comfortable
		◯ 89% and Below = Difficult

Reading Comprehension and Personal Reading Record • Emergent Learner—Grades K–1

Student Name _____ Grade _____ School Year _____

READING COMPREHENSION

Date* _____ Teacher Comments

Literal
- Details ....
- Pronoun Reference ....
- Sequence ....

Inferential
- Relate To Personal Experiences ..
- Main Idea ....
- Cause/Effect ....
- Draw Conclusions ....
- Predict Outcomes ....
- Compare/Contrast ....

Critical Thinking
- Analyze Character ....
- Real/Make-Believe ....

<u>Additional Comments:</u>

PERSONAL READING

Date* _____ Teacher Comments

Observation
- Chooses To Read ....
- Selects Appropriate Books ....

<u>Additional Comments:</u>

* May wish to record once each instructional quarter of the school year

Reading Comprehension and Personal Reading CLASS PROFILE
Emergent Learners (Grades K–1)

Teacher _____

Year _____

NAME	Details	Pronoun Reference	Sequence	Relate To Personal Experiences	Main Idea	Cause/Effect	Draw Conclusions	Predict Outcomes	Compare/Contrast	Analyze Character	Real/Make-Believe	Chooses To Read	Selects Appropriate Books
	LITERAL COMPREHENSION			INFERENTIAL COMPREHENSION					CRITICAL THINKING			PERSONAL READING	
1.													
2.													
3.													
4.													
5.													
6.													
7.													
8.													
9.													
10.													
11.													
12.													
13.													
14.													
15.													
16.													
17.													
18.													
19.													
20.													
21.													
22.													
23.													
24.													
25.													
26.													
27.													
28.													
29.													
30.													

Reading Comprehension and Personal Reading Record • Developing Learner—Grades 2-3

Student Name _____ Grade _____ School Year _____

READING COMPREHENSION

Date*   Teacher Comments

Literal
- Details.............................
- Pronoun Reference.............
- Sequence..........................

Inferential
- Relate To Personal Experiences ..
- Main Idea ....
- Cause/Effect.......................
- Draw Conclusions ....
- Predict Outcomes ....
- Compare/Contrast...............

Critical Thinking
- Analyze Character ....
- Real/Make-Believe ....
- Summarize Plot ....

Additional Comments:

PERSONAL READING

Date*   Teacher Comments

Observation
- Chooses To Read ....
- Selects Appropriate Books .....

Discussion
- Aware of Author/Illustrator.........

Additional Comments:

* May wish to record once each instructional quarter of the school year

©1995 by Incentive Publications, Inc., Nashville, TN.

Reading Comprehension and Personal Reading
CLASS PROFILE
Developing Learners (Grades 2–3)

Teacher _____

Year _____

NAME	Details	Pronoun Reference	Sequence	Relate To Personal Experiences	Main Idea	Cause/Effect	Draw Conclusions	Predict Outcomes	Compare/Contrast	Analyze Character	Real/Make-Believe	Summarize Plot	Chooses To Read	Selects Appropriate Books	Aware of Author/Illustrator
	LITERAL COMPREHENSION			INFERENTIAL COMPREHENSION						CRITICAL THINKING			PERSONAL READING		
1.															
2.															
3.															
4.															
5.															
6.															
7.															
8.															
9.															
10.															
11.															
12.															
13.															
14.															
15.															
16.															
17.															
18.															
19.															
20.															
21.															
22.															
23.															
24.															
25.															
26.															
27.															
28.															
29.															
30.															

Reading Comprehension and Personal Reading Record • Fluent Learner—Grades 4–6

Student Name _____   Grade ____   School Year ____

READING COMPREHENSION

	*Date**			*Teacher Comments*

Literal
- Details..................
- Pronoun Reference..............
- Sequence.................

Inferential
- Relate To Personal Experiences ..
- Main Idea ....
- Cause/Effect...............
- Draw Conclusions ....
- Predict Outcomes..........
- Compare/Contrast..........

Critical Thinking
- Analyze Character/Setting........
- Summarize Plot ....
- Fact/Opinion...............
- Mood..................
- Author's Tone/Intent............

Additional Comments:

PERSONAL READING

	*Date**			*Teacher Comments*

Observation
- Chooses To Read ....
- Selects Appropriate Books ....

Discussion
- Aware of Author/Illustrator.........
- Selects Books By Subject............

Additional Comments:

* *May wish to record once each instructional quarter of the school year*

©1995 by Incentive Publications, Inc., Nashville, TN.

Reading Comprehension and Personal Reading
CLASS PROFILE
Fluent Learners (Grades 4-6)

Teacher _____

Year _____

NAME	Details	Pronoun Reference	Sequence	Relate To Personal Experiences	Main Idea	Cause/Effect	Draw Conclusions	Predict Outcomes	Compare/Contrast	Analyze Character	Summarize Plot	Fact/Opinion	Mood	Author's Tone/Intent	Chooses To Read	Selects Appropriate Books	Aware of Author/Illustrator	Selects Books By Subject
	LITERAL COMPREHENSION			**INFERENTIAL COMPREHENSION**						**CRITICAL THINKING**					**PERSONAL READING**			
1.																		
2.																		
3.																		
4.																		
5.																		
6.																		
7.																		
8.																		
9.																		
10.																		
11.																		
12.																		
13.																		
14.																		
15.																		
16.																		
17.																		
18.																		
19.																		
20.																		
21.																		
22.																		
23.																		
24.																		
25.																		
26.																		
27.																		
28.																		
29.																		
30.																		

Chapter Eight

PERFORMANCE ASSESSMENT

Performance assessment is a method of evaluating students through their performance on "classwork-like" assignments. Unlike standardized testing procedures that stop the student's regular routine to administer tests using an unfamiliar format, performance assessment maintains the class routine using a format familiar to all students. Because of this, performance assessment is gaining popularity.

The whole language classroom involves students in all aspects of reading, writing, listening, and speaking; therefore, there exists a need to evaluate effectively the depth and breadth of all of these processes. Performance assessment accomplishes this through *embedded, on demand, enhanced,* and *justified* testing practices.

Embedded
Teachers evaluate student progress for their own information. Assessment is embedded in regular instruction.

On Demand
Districts administer a standard assessment at specific times during the year.

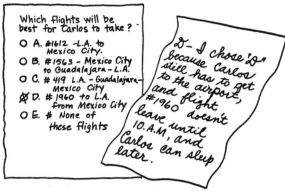

Enhanced

Multiple choice tests that interpret many forms of information at one time—maps, charts, graphs, tables, and reading passages. Because high-level thinking processes are involved, this process is considered enhanced.

Justified

Multiple choice tests in which all choices are correct, but the student justifies his or her answers in written form.

These forms of performance assessment represent the best way to evaluate real learning since they are based on the types of choices people must make in the real world. Whole language teachers use *embedded* assessment continually. In fact, this entire book is dedicated to various forms of embedded evaluation—informal assessment, portfolios, observation and notation, reading records, and conferencing. Districts have used *on demand* evaluation for decades, usually in the form of standardized tests. Now, however, a form of performance assessment is becoming widely used in district testing procedures, as well. *Enhanced* multiple choice tests are being closely examined by companies that publish standardized tests. Departments of education in a few states are field testing both enhanced and *justified* assessments. The justified multiple choice tests are best applied to fluent speakers in intermediate or middle grades (4th, 5th, and 6th). Once teachers and students adapt to the idea of enhanced testing, all subject areas (reading, math, science, social studies) can be assessed in this way.

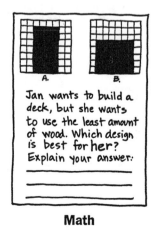

Math

Science

Social Studies

As performance assessment gains popularity, more and more teachers and districts will discover its relevance to actual classroom learning and adapt it to fit their individual evaluation needs.

EXAMPLES OF PERFORMANCE ASSESSMENTS AND SCORING RUBRICS

Below are examples of performance assessments for each developmental learning level: emergent (grades K–1), developing (grades 2–3), and fluent (grades 4–6). Note that all of the activities are based on a literature book or passage. They involve many of the reading and writing concepts outlined on the *Scope and Sequence Chart of Whole Language Skills*, pages 13–14. There are no right or wrong answers to correct. Evaluation is based on a scoring rubric developed for each skill level. These assessments can be used as either embedded or on demand assessments. Districts may decide to administer on demand performance assessments two or three time a year. The most logical time to give them is at the end of each teaching quarter.

On Demand Assessment Schedule

	1st Quarter	2nd Quarter	3rd Quarter	4th Quarter
Twice A Year	X		X	
Three Times A Year	X	X	X	

It is best to have completed the assessment by the end of the third quarter so that teachers and parents have time to make decisions about a child's progress. By the end of the fourth quarter little can be done to improve a student's progress.

PERFORMANCE ASSESSMENT FOR EMERGENT LEARNERS

This is a three-day sample performance assessment based on *The Carrot Seed* by Ruth Krauss. Each day's session lasts approximately 45 minutes. It is recommended that the teacher duplicate and distribute the pages a day at a time. (Reproducible forms for this sample assessment are on pages 124–130.) This assessment is intended for children with some writing skills. It is not recommended for beginning kindergartners.

Day One: Predicting, Reading Book, Sequencing Events, Copying and Completing Sentence Frame

Before-Reading Activities: Discuss the title and cover of the book and how the story might begin and end. Write student predictions on the chalkboard under the headings: "Begin" and "End." Read aloud the phrases with the students, pointing to each word.

Begin	End
He plants a seed.	It gets wet.
He puts it in a hole.	It makes a carrot.
The seed goes in the dirt.	It grows very big.
He watches it go down.	He waits and waits.

Read Aloud: Read aloud *The Carrot Seed*. Direct the students to listen to what happens in the beginning and end of the story.

After-Reading Activity: Ask the students what happened at the beginning of the story and what happened at the end. Reread the sentences on the chalkboard together with the students. Discuss which sentences best describe what happened first in the story and circle them. Then discuss which sentences best describe what happened at the end of the story and circle them.

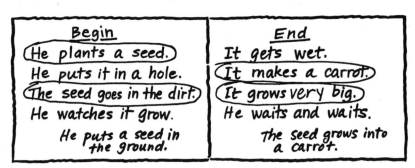

Write the appropriate sentences under the headings "First the boy . . ." and "In the end . . ." on a piece of chart paper. Read each sentence with the class. Have the students supply other phrases to correctly complete each sentence frame.

(Note: Keep the chart paper to use again in the third day of the assessment.)

First the boy _____.	In the end _____.
plants a seed.	a carrot grows.
puts a seed in the ground.	the seed grows into a carrot.
drops a seed in the dirt.	a plant grows very big.
	he gets a big carrot.
	a big carrot grew.

Writing Assignment: On page 2 and 3 of the performance assessment, the students complete each sentence frame: "First the boy . . ." and "In the end . . . ." They can either copy a phrase from each chart or write their own sentences. Then they can draw pictures to illustrate each one. The students should not receive help with their spelling or punctuation. How the writing appears is an indication of the level at which a child's reading and writing abilities are functioning.

Evaluation: Listen to each student read what he or she has written while pointing to each word. Keep each student's paper and make a notation stating whether or not the student can do this, and then assign each paper a number from the scoring rubric on page 117.

Day Two: Reading Book, Cause/Effect Relationships, Copying and Completing Sentences

Before-Reading Activity: Ask students to recall from yesterday's activities what happened at the beginning and end of the story. Then instruct them to listen to what the little boy did to make the carrot seed grow.

Read Aloud: Read aloud *The Carrot Seed* again. The students will listen for what the little boy did to the carrot seed to make it grow.

After-Reading Activity: Ask the students what the little boy did to make the carrot seed grow. Write a sentence frame and then record their responses on chart paper. Read aloud with the students the sentence frame, inserting each phrase and pointing to each word as it is read. Then discuss the types of things that could have happened if it didn't grow. Write a sentence frame and list student responses on chart paper. Read the sentence frame with the students, completing it with each phrase written below it and pointing to each word as you read it aloud.

Writing Assignment: On pages 4 and 5 of the performance assessment, the students will complete each sentence frame by copying a phrase from each chart or writing their own sentences. Then they can illustrate their work. Again, no assistance should be given with spelling or punctuation, as errors reveal a great deal of information about students' ability levels.

```
To make it grow he —
    put it in dirt.
    pulled weeds.
    watered it.
```

```
It will not grow if—
    it is not in dirt.
    weeds grow.
    there is no water.
    it does not get water.
```

Evaluation: Listen to students individually read their writing, then note on their papers if they can point to each word as they read. Keep student papers and assign them numbers from the scoring rubric on page 117.

(Note: Chart papers should be kept for the next day's assessment.)

Day Three: Reading Book, Drawing Conclusions, Beginning Reference Skills, Writing Original Sentences

Before-Reading Activity: Ask students to remember yesterday's discussion about what the little boy did to the plant to make it grow. Then instruct them to listen to the story one more time for clues about the different things plants need to grow.

Read Aloud: Read aloud *The Carrot Seed* again. The students will listen for clues about what plants need to grow.

After-Reading Activity: Ask students to draw conclusions from the story about what plants need to grow. List student responses on a piece of chart paper. Read aloud each phrase together, pointing to each word as it is read. Have students volunteer sentences they could write from this information.

```
Plants need _____.
  dirt
  water
  weeds pulled
  sunshine
  someone to care for it
```

(Note: Teachers may wish to put up charts from the last two days and ask students to write everything they know about the story *The Carrot Seed*. This activity is well-suited for the experienced first grader.)

Writing Assignment: On pages 6 and 7 of the performance assessment, students either complete the sentence frame or write their own sentences. Allow them to spell and punctuate on their own.

Evaluation: Listen to students read their writing and note whether or not they can point to each word as it is read. File their papers with their other writing on *The Carrot Seed* and assign a cumulative score from the scoring rubric below.

(Note: Enter each day's score and final score on the front page of the Emergent Performance Assessment. Write any pertinent comments there, as well.)

Emergent Learners' Scoring Rubric

1 Needs Developmental Work	2 Working At Level	3 Becoming A Developing Learner
• Scribbles, writes, or uses strings of letters • Writes some beginning letters • Has difficulty copying from the board • Unable to sequence events	• Spaces words properly in sentence • Invented spelling includes correct beginning and ending letters • Writes own simple sentences • Sequences two events	• Invented spelling includes correct beginning, middle, and ending letters • Spells some commonly used words correctly • Writes two or more original sentences (more complex) • Sequences three or more events

This is a three-day sample performance assessment based on the book *Patrick's Dinosaurs* by Carol Carrick. Each day's session lasts approximately 45 minutes.

It is recommended that the teacher duplicate and distribute the full three-day packet of student pages to the class and collect them at the end of each day's session. Reproducible forms for the assessment are provided on pages 131–135.

Day One: Reading, Predicting Outcomes, Story Details, Real/Make-Believe

Before-Reading Activity: Discuss the title and cover of the book, then ask students what dinosaurs might be in the story. Students record their thoughts on the "Day One: Before-Reading" section of the performance assessment packet. After students have recorded their ideas, direct them to read the "After-Reading" questions. Tell them to read the story with these questions in mind.

Read Story: Students read *Patrick's Dinosaurs*. (You may wish to read aloud the story to the class if their reading skills do not allow them to comprehend it on their own.) Either way, the entire class should have access to the story the same way—either they read it themselves, or they listen as it is read to them.)

After-Reading Activity: Students draw and write about four dinosaurs in the story on the "Day One: After-Reading" sheet. Discuss what was real and make-believe in the story and ask students to list their own thoughts.

Day Two: Group Work on Main Ideas, Story Details, Compare/Contrast

Cooperative Reading Activity: In cooperative groups of four or five students, each student rereads the story and brainstorms ideas to answer the "Day Two" questions in their performance assessment packet.

Day Three: Compare/Contrast, Organizing Information for Paragraphs

Before-Reading Activity: Students individually review the cooperative group activity completed the day before. Lead a discussion of their responses, paying particular attention to attributes of each dinosaur and to their similarities and differences. Instruct the students to reread the story to gain information about the two dinosaurs they compared and contrasted the day before so that they can now write a report about them.

Read Story: Students read *Patrick's Dinosaurs.*

Writing Activity: Students write about their individual choices of two dinosaurs on the last page of their performance assessment packet. Encourage them to use their notes made the day before in the cooperative group exercise.

Evaluation: Evaluation of the assessment takes place at either the school or district level. Teachers at each grade level meet to score each student's work according to the developing learners' scoring rubric on page 120. Two different teachers score each student's paper. If the two teachers' scores differ by two or more points, a third teacher will read and assign the determining score.

Evaluation Process

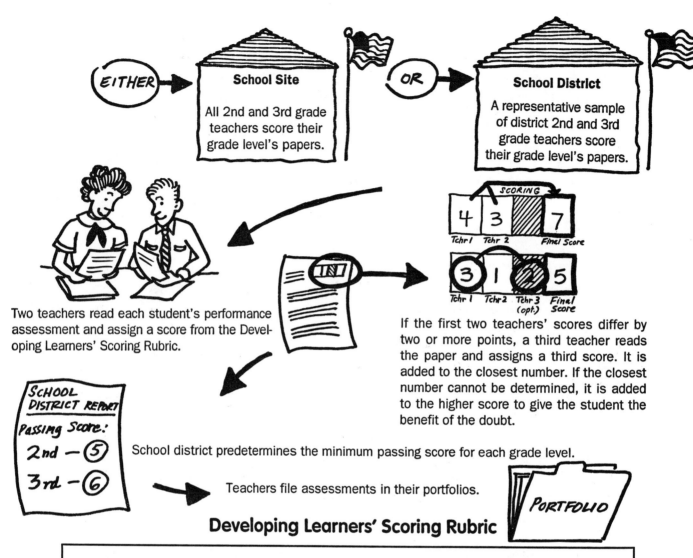

EITHER → **School Site** — All 2nd and 3rd grade teachers score their grade level's papers.

OR → **School District** — A representative sample of district 2nd and 3rd grade teachers score their grade level's papers.

SCORING

4	3		7
Tchr 1	Tchr 2		Final Score

3	1	0	5
Tchr 1	Tchr 2	Tchr 3 (opt.)	Final Score

Two teachers read each student's performance assessment and assign a score from the Developing Learners' Scoring Rubric.

If the first two teachers' scores differ by two or more points, a third teacher reads the paper and assigns a third score. It is added to the closest number. If the closest number cannot be determined, it is added to the higher score to give the student the benefit of the doubt.

SCHOOL DISTRICT REPORT
Passing Score:
2nd — ⑤
3rd — ⑥

School district predetermines the minimum passing score for each grade level.

Teachers file assessments in their portfolios.

PORTFOLIO

Developing Learners' Scoring Rubric

5—Sentences vary in length and complexity. Uses vivid words and conventional spelling, capitalization, and punctuation. Shows exceptional understanding of story and goes beyond details to show insight into character or factual information.

4—Sentences show a good degree of complexity. Spells most words correctly. Most capitalization and punctuation rules observed. Shows very good understanding of story, and uses details when revealing character or relating factual information.

3—Sentences are of average length and complexity. Spells many words correctly. Basic capitalization and punctuation rules observed. Story details understood enough to reveal character or factual information.

2—Sentences vary between simple and slightly more complex. Some words spelled correctly; otherwise, uses invented spelling. Some capitalization and punctuation mistakes. Basic story details somewhat understood.

1—Sentence structure is simple. Uses only invented spelling and little capitalization and punctuation. Few story details understood.

0—Unable to complete task.

PERFORMANCE ASSESSMENT FOR FLUENT LEARNERS

This is a three-day sample performance assessment based on an excerpt from the book *The Island of the Blue Dolphins* by Scott O'Dell. Each day's session lasts from 45 minutes to an hour. It is recommended that the teacher duplicate and distribute the full three-day packet of student pages to the class and collect them at the end of each day's session. Reproducible forms for this sample performance assessment are provided on pages 136–143.

Day One: Reading, Predicting Outcomes, Main Idea, Story Details, Drawing Conclusions, Relating Story To Personal Experiences

Before-Reading Activity: Distribute the excerpt from Chapter 9 of *The Island of the Blue Dolphins* which begins "For many days I did not think of the weapons again, not until the wild dogs came one night and sat under the rock and howled . . ." and ends "Yet every night I climbed onto the rock to sleep."
Ask students to read the preface on the cover page of their performance assessment and complete the "Before-Reading" section of the packet.

Read Passage: Students read the passage from *The Island of the Blue Dolphins*.

After-Reading Activity: Students complete the questions about the passage.

Day Two: Brainstorming, Using Vivid Words, Character Analysis, Drawing Conclusions, Cause/Effect Relationships

Small Group Activity: In small groups of four or five, students reread the passage, brainstorm, and complete the next set of questions.

Day Three: Writing, Organizing Ideas, Mechanics

Writing Activity: Students use the map from yesterday's group activity. Encourage them to add to it if they wish to organize their thoughts before writing. They are to write a diary entry from Karana's point of view explaining why she did not make weapons and what happened as a result of her decision. Remind them to use vivid words along with correct capitalization and punctuation. Then give students time to write their stories.

Evaluation: Evaluation takes place at the district level where a representative sample of teachers from each grade level reads and scores that grade level's papers. Two teachers read each student's paper and give two scores according to the scoring rubric on page 123—one for reading and one for writing. If either of the teachers' scores differ by two or more points, a third teacher reads the paper and makes the final determination. These scores can help teachers diagnose and address student weaknesses. The scores may also be used as minimum requirements for passing or retaining students in the middle grades.

The Evaluation Process

Representative samples of 4th, 5th, and 6th grade teachers score their grade level's papers. (Note: Set aside a full day per grade level for scoring. Example: 4th grade on Tuesday, 5th grade on Wednesday, 6th grade on Thursday.)

Two teachers read each student's paper and assign both a reading and a writing score.

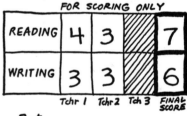

FOR SCORING ONLY

	Tchr 1	Tchr 2	Tch 3	FINAL SCORE
READING	4	3		7
WRITING	3	3		6

But....

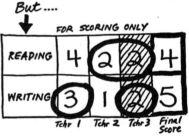

FOR SCORING ONLY

	Tchr 1	Tchr 2	Tchr 3	Final Score
READING	4	2	2	4
WRITING	3	1	2	5

The school district predetermines the minimum passing score for each grade level and subject (reading and writing).

If either score differs by two or more points, a third teacher reads the paper and assigns a score. It is added to the nearest or closest score. If the nearest score cannot be determined, add it to the higher score to give the student the benefit of the doubt.

PASSING SCORE

4th — Reading — 5 / Writing — 4
5th — Reading — 6 / Writing — 4
6th — Reading — 6 / Writing — 5

PORTFOLIO

Teachers file the performance assessments in student portfolios for next year's teacher.

Fluent Learners' Scoring Rubric

Reading

5 — *Excellent*. Exceptional understanding of passage. Gleans unusual insight from ideas conveyed and extends them beyond the confines of the test. May even challenge aspects of the passage.

4 — *Commendable*. Shows a very good understanding of passage significance. Extends and applies knowledge, but level of intensity may vary among questions.

3 — *Average*. Understands significance of text beyond basic comprehension. Gives accurate summary of facts. Makes some extensions and applications.

2 — *Fair*. Basic literal comprehension, but little else. Can retell plot, but with some inaccuracies.

1 — *Poor*. Little sense of basic comprehension. Factual errors apparent. Copies information from text.

0 — *Fail*. Unable to complete task.

Writing

5 — *Excellent*. Exceptional organization and command of written language. Uses vivid, compelling sentences. No errors in spelling, grammar, or punctuation.

4 — *Commendable*. Sentences show a good degree of complexity and are correctly written. Very good organization of ideas. Few errors, if any, in spelling, grammar, or punctuation.

3 — *Average*. Sentences are of regular length and complexity. Minor organizational flaws, but ideas flow logically. Some errors in sentence structure, grammar, spelling, or punctuation.

2 — *Fair*. Sentences show little variety. Some sense of organization evident, but focus is unclear. Several errors in sentence structure, grammar, spelling, or punctuation.

1 — *Poor*. No sentence variety. No evidence of organization or focus. Many errors in sentence structure, spelling, grammar, or punctuation.

0 — *Fail*. Unable to complete task.

Emergent Performance Assessment

GRADE 1

The Carrot Seed
.by Ruth Kraus

	Day 1	Day 2	Day 3	Final Score
Score				
Comments				

Name _____ Date _____

Teacher _____

School _____

PERFORMANCE ASSESSMENT—GRADE 1

DAY ONE Writing Lesson

First the boy

DAY ONE   Writing Lesson

In the end

DAY TWO   Writing Lesson

To make it grow he

DAY TWO   Writing Lesson

It will not grow if

DAY THREE   Writing Lesson

Plants need

DAY THREE   Writing Lesson

Developing Learner Performance Assessment

GRADE 3

Patrick's Dinosaurs
by Carol Carrick

For Scoring Only

Teacher 1	Teacher 2	Teacher 3 (optional)	Final Score

Name _____ Date _____

Teacher _____

School _____

DAY ONE: Before-Reading Activity

Why do you think the story is called *Patrick's Dinosaurs?*

_____

_____

_____

_____

What dinosaurs do you think will be in the story?

DAY ONE   After-Reading Activity

Draw and write about four dinosaurs in the story.

Write about some real and make-believe things in the story. Draw them.

REAL	**MAKE-BELIEVE**

PERFORMANCE ASSESSMENT—GRADE 3

DAY TWO   Group Activity

What other title would you give this story? Explain your answer.

_____

_____

_____

Draw and write everything you know about these dinosaurs from the story.

Brontosaurus

Crocodile

_____

_____

_____

_____

_____

_____

Diplodocus

Stegosaurus

_____

_____

_____

_____

_____

_____

PERFORMANCE ASSESSMENT—GRADE 3

DAY TWO   Group Activity

Draw and write everything you know about these dinosaurs from the story.

Triceratops	**Tyrannosaurus Rex**

_____   _____

_____   _____

_____   _____

Choose two dinosaurs from the story. Write and draw to show ways in which they are the same and different. My two dinosaurs are:

_____   _____

SAME	**DIFFERENT**

_____   _____

_____   _____

_____   _____

DAY THREE   Group Activity

Use your notes from yesterday's activity and write everything you know about the two dinosaurs you chose.

_____

(Title)

_____

_____

_____

_____

_____

_____

_____

_____

_____

_____

_____

_____

_____

_____

_____

_____

_____

_____

Turn your paper over to illustrate your work.

135

Fluent Learner Performance Assessment

GRADE 5

Island of the Blue Dolphins
by Scott O'Dell

For Scoring Only

	Teacher 1	Teacher 2	Teacher 3 (optional)	Final Score
Reading				
Writing				

Name _____ Date _____

Teacher _____

School _____ Grade_____

DAY ONE: Before-Reading Activity

Karana is an Indian girl who was left behind on an island when her tribe sailed away. Her young brother, Ramo, was with her until he was killed by a pack of wild dogs that roamed the island. Now she is alone and without weapons to defend herself.

Though she sleeps on a high rock where the wild dogs cannot get at her, they watch her and she feels afraid.

Women in her tribe were not allowed to make weapons. But now Karana must make a choice between her safety and the beliefs of her tribe.

Turn the page and complete the "Before-Reading" section.

DAY ONE   Before-Reading Activity

What are some questions you have about the passage you are about to read?

_____

_____

_____

_____

_____

What do you think you would do if you were Karana? _____

_____

_____

_____

_____

_____

Why do you think her tribe doesn't want women to make weapons?_____

_____

_____

_____

_____

_____

What do you think might happen if Karana makes weapons? _____

_____

_____

_____

_____

_____

DAY ONE   After-Reading Activity

Write what you know about these characters after reading the passage.

Karana	Wild Dogs	Ramo
_____	_____	_____
_____	_____	_____
_____	_____	_____
_____	_____	_____

Draw and label the parts of the weapons Karana made.

Write the thoughts that might have been going through Karana's head when she chose to make weapons.

| DAY ONE   After-Reading Activity |

What title would you give this passage? Explain your answer._____

_____
_____
_____
_____

Read this sentence and give an example of this from your own life.
   Karana had watched her father make weapons; however, she says she "had watched, but not with the eye of one who would ever do it."

Write an example from your life. _____

_____
_____
_____
_____

Choose from the passage a sentence you especially liked and write it.

_____
_____
_____

Why did you choose this sentence?_____

_____
_____
_____
_____
_____

DAY TWO   Group Work

Brainstorm words that best describe these characters.

Karana

Wild Dogs

What is the main issue Karana must solve in this passage? _____

_____

_____

_____

Brainstorm other ways Karana could have solved her problem. _____

_____

_____

_____

_____

Write the thoughts that might have been going through Karana's head if she had decided not to make weapons.

_____

_____

_____

_____

_____

_____

DAY TWO   Group Work

Brainstorm words to describe how Karana might have felt if she had not made any weapons.

_____

_____

Tomorrow, you will write about why Karana did not make any weapons and what happened as a result of her decision.

Fill in this map to organize your ideas. Do not use any help to complete it.

KARANA

PROBLEM:

SOLUTION:

Not to make weapons because _____

_____

_____

WHAT HAPPENED AS A RESULT?

_____

_____

_____

_____

_____

DAY TWO   Group Work

Take turns sharing your map in your group. Add any ideas you get from your group to the idea cloud below.

DAY THREE Writing

Pretend you are Karana. Write in your diary what your problem was, why you decided not to make weapons, and what happened as a result.

Diary

Chapter Nine

COMMUNICATING
WITH PARENTS

Since whole language differs from the traditional basal approach to learning, it is very important to keep open the lines of communication with parents. Parents will, understandably, have many questions about the daily class routine and how their child is progressing in it. As a result, teachers will need to spend time explaining student progress in commonly understood language. Parents don't care if their child is emergent, developing, or fluent, they just want to know if their child is learning at a normal rate and if any specific problems need to be addressed.

Parents tend to judge their children's classroom experience by their own elementary and middle school experiences. The vast majority of them are familiar with traditional basal programs, and the idea of literature-based reading coupled with writing instead of workbook assignments is a foreign concept. For the whole language process to be understood by parents, the teacher needs to consistently educate parents about the basic components of whole language.

Literature-Based Program	Many Reading, Writing, Listening, and Speaking Experiences	Thematic Units are the mode of instruction.	= WHOLE LANGUAGE

A good time to introduce parents to a whole language program is at a Back-To-School Night during the first month of the school year. There, the ideas of literature-based instruction, fewer worksheets and more reading, writing, listening, and speaking experiences, and the year's thematic units can be explained to parents. Thereafter, a biweekly or monthly newsletter can offer more insight into the class's whole language experiences. Periodically sending home student portfolios along with explanations of developing spelling, sentence, and paragraph mechanics will illustrate each student's development in reading, writing, math, science, and social studies.

Parent conferences, of course, offer an excellent opportunity to share information on a child's growth and development. However, by the time parent conferences occur, parents should be well-versed in the basic structure of the whole language classroom. Explaining whole language to thirty-five separate sets of parents is not an effective use of conference time. Holding quarterly "Family Nights" throughout the year, however, can culminate a unit and involve the whole family in the learning process. Last, but not least, report cards provide a good overview of each student's abilities in language parents can readily understand.

BACK-TO-SCHOOL NIGHT

Chances are Back-To-School Night will be the first opportunity a teacher has to meet face-to-face with all or most of his or her class's parents. This is a good time to explain all aspects of the classroom program and outline the goals and themes for the year. Samples of concepts to introduce during a Back-To-School Night program are detailed below.

SAMPLE BACK-TO-SCHOOL NIGHT PROGRAM

Listening and Speaking
- Listening Posts
- Puppets, play clothes
- Teacher reads aloud daily
- Sharing time
- Oral reports
- Recording original stories
- Performing plays, character studies, puppet shows
- Small group projects

Reading
- Big books/predictable books/pocket charts
- Decoding skills/phonics
- Sight words
- Silent reading daily
- Take-home books
- Research

Writing
- Dictating stories
- Completing sentence frames
- Invented/conventional spelling
- Original stories
- Paragraphs
- Organizing ideas
- Poetry
- Editing

Math
- Manipulatives
- Basic computational skills
- Geometry
- Numeration concepts
- Measurement
- Maps, charts, graphs, diagrams

Science/Social Studies
- Year's themes to be studied
- Field trips and learning experiences planned

Evaluation Process
- Portfolios
- Informal assessments
- Reading records and conferences
- Performance assessments
- Observations
- Standardized tests

District Minimums
- Distribute district minimums

Parent Involvement
- Volunteers
- Items for "wish list"
- Newsletter

A class newsletter sent home every other week or each month is an excellent way of keeping parents apprised of what's going on in the classroom. The newsletter can explain new concepts, such as what to expect with invented spelling or semantic mapping. It can also recommend good books for gift-giving and birthdays. Wish lists of items the teacher needs for the next unit of study, along with some facts about the next theme to be studied, are great newsletter additions.

Parent volunteers can type the final copy of the newsletter so that the teacher's time can be better spent planning. Volunteer middle grade students can also help prepare the final newsletter.

Examples of appropriate newsletter items are included below.

Invented Spelling
Beginning writers use invented spelling before conventional spelling. This is a normal learning process. Invented spelling tells us a great deal about a child's learning process. Here are some examples of the writing you may see:

mwm — Scribbles or strings of letters show a child knows that writing is a way to communicate.

i wts — (I went to the store.) Child knows beginning sounds.

i can se — (I can see.) Child knows there are spaces between words and knows beginning, ending, and some middle sounds.

Each is an important step in learning the steps of reading and writing.

New Theme—All About Me
We are beginning a new theme. It will deal with our families, friends, and feelings. Our first project will be . . .

**Emergent Learners
(Grades K–1)**

"Mapping" Ideas
We are learning to organize ideas into paragraphs. To begin, we need a "map" of ideas. Below is an example.

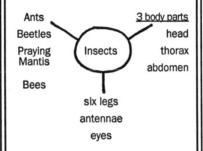

From these maps we can write one-paragraph reports. Each part of the map becomes a sentence.

Parent Night
Tuesday evening at 7:00 p.m. parents are invited to learn more about "mapping" ideas. We will also discuss some beginning research projects based on our upcoming theme.

**Developing Learners
(Grades 2–3)**

Persuasive Writing
Persuasive writing is a powerful tool. We are studying how newspaper columns and magazine ads use persuasive writing to make their points. Then we will write our own newspaper columns and magazine ads.

Our next project will be to make radio and TV ads after we have studied them. Your children will be asked to listen to the radio and watch TV for the persuasive methods used.

Family Night
To culminate our Persuasive Writing unit, we will air our audio tapes and videos along with a class magazine of columns and ads for you to see. Come join us, Wednesday, April 16 at 7:00 p.m.

Wish List
We need these items for our unit:
- daily newspapers
- magazines
- tape recorders
- audio tapes

**Fluent Learners
(Grades 4–6)**

Parent volunteers are an integral part of the classroom, as their assistance keeps the program operating smoothly and efficiently. While not all parents and guardians can contribute to the classroom, most can give some portion of their time, either at school for the whole class or at home for their own child. Send home a letter detailing the type of help parents can contribute. You may want to use the reproducible form on page 148 or create one to suit your own needs.

Dear Parent(s)/Caretaker(s):

There are many ways to volunteer your time to the classroom. Below are listed a few. If you can think of other ways to invest your time, let me know. Please sign your name and the type of volunteering you are willing to do, and return the bottom portion of the form to me.

Thanks!

Volunteer on a weekly basis.

Volunteer a lunch hour a week/bi-weekly to read aloud to kids.

Prepare class projects/newsletters at home.

Give 15-minute book talks periodically.

Participate in one class project.

Donate needed materials to school.

Drive on one or more fieldtrips.

Organize local businesses to donate time/material for projects.

Select/organize library books around a theme being studied.

Record tapes for listening center at home.

Spearhead parent drive to buy a class set of needed books.

Do the legwork for organizing a fieldtrip.

Cut and return to teacher.

_____ can volunteer by_____ on
(Parent's/Caregiver's Name)   (activity)

_____ Signed_____
(dates/days)

Telephone: Home _____ Work _____

Parents can achieve an accurate understanding of how their children are doing in school by either reading to their children or listening to them read. Children take home book bags containing a book and a note the parents will sign indicating either that they read to their child or listened to the child read to them.

| **Emergent Learners**
(Grades K–1) | **Developing Learners**
(Grades 2–3) | **Fluent Learners**
(Grades 4–6) |

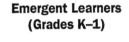

Parent reads aloud to child.   Child reads book aloud to three people.   Child reads chapter aloud to parents.

In a newsletter, teachers can point out appropriate questions parents should ask their children or topics they should discuss about the take-home reading. In the case of take-home portfolios, the teacher can include a questionnaire the parents fill out with their child.

Periodically the teacher and students should examine one of the child's portfolios (Writing, Math/Science/Social Studies, or Showcase) and choose two or three samples to take home and share with parents. Together, the child and parent review the child's work and complete the *Take-Home Portfolio Questionnaire* (pages 153–154). This gives parents insight into their child's work they could receive no other way.

PARENT CONFERENCES

Parent conferences are excellent times to meet with parents and discuss their child's progress in school. To use this time most effectively, teachers may wish to send home the *Parent Questions for Parent Conferencing* sheet (page 155) a few days before conferences. This form helps parents formulate their questions and helps the teacher make sure he or she has covered everything.

By the time parent conferences occur, the parents should have a basic understanding of the whole language program through Back-To-School Night, newsletters, take-home books, and portfolio samples. That basis of understanding makes conferencing a time when the parents and teacher discuss the child, rather than a time when the entire whole language program is explained. A child's portfolio can speak volumes about the whole language process; however, avoid displaying the showcase portfolio at parent conferences. It does not reveal a child's real growth the way that the writing or math/science/social studies portfolios would. The showcase portfolio is better displayed at Open House or Family Nights.

It is also important to speak to parents using terms they understand. Words like "emergent," "developing," "fluent," and "performance assessment" mean little to them and often serve to confuse and alienate them from tracking their child's progress. Just like doctors and engineers, teachers have developed a specialized language that most people do not understand. It is important to be conscious of that when meeting with parents. As well, parents should not be overwhelmed with too many bits of information. Have the child's report card completed, or write all important information about the child's progress on one or two pieces of paper. If the parents ask for more information, look it up in your anecdotal records or other files you have on hand.

In other words, keep parent conferences simple and straightforward. Discuss the child's strengths and weaknesses in plain English, and do your homework so the child's progress is reflected on the report card or another sheet of paper.

Send home parent questionnaire and audio tape of child reading aloud before a conference.

Speak in plain English and have report card filled out and child's portfolios available.

Have available anecdotal records and other files, but don't waste time rummaging through them during the conference, unless necessary.

Parent Night or Family Night is a great forum in which to culminate a unit the class has been studying or introduce a new whole language concept to parents. Host a Parent Night or Family Night once each quarter to keep parents apprised of what is happening in their child's classroom.

At Parent Night, parents are invited to the classroom for one evening to learn about only one aspect of a whole language program or to hear a speaker discuss whole language or some other aspect of the classroom.

Emergent Learners
(Grades K–1)

Developing Learners
(Grades 2–3)

Fluent Learners
(Grades 4–6)

Family Nights are times when the entire family (parents, children, and siblings) are invited to observe or participate in the culminating activity of a class unit.

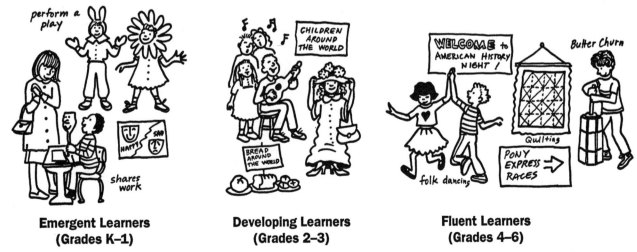

Emergent Learners
(Grades K–1)

Developing Learners
(Grades 2–3)

Fluent Learners
(Grades 4–6)

Everyone becomes part of the learning during Parent Night or Family Night, and these types of occasions help strengthen the whole language process as well as secure the bond of communication between home and school.

Report cards, of course, are another means of communicating to parents about their child. Whatever form the report card takes, it should provide a good overview of student abilities in plain language that parents can understand. Parents should not be put in the position of having to learn teacher jargon to understand how their child is doing in school. Since the whole purpose of the report card is to tell parents about their child, it needs to be easily understood.

Another recommendation is to avoid giving letter grades to primary children (grades K–3). Since their basic skills are still developing, they don't need the added pressure of grades. Assigning letter grades is fine for fluent learners (grades 4–6).

WHERE ARE THE STUDENTS IN ALL OF THIS?

The student is an integral part of the entire whole language process and is an especially important link in communicating the ideas of the whole language program to parents. Students have input into the work that goes in their portfolios and can see their own progress as they witness the growth of their work. Their increased fluency in reading can be heard on the audio tapes of them periodically reading aloud.

The basic assumption that children are natural learners who want to read and write is the foundation on which whole language is based. By letting those natural learning processes of listening and speaking form the basis of the reading and writing that students do, teachers and parents have an important key in the pursuit of national literacy which will guarantee a fruitful future for all children.*

*For more information about establishing and teaching a whole language program, refer to *Everything You Need To Know To Be a Successful Whole Language Teacher* by Judith Cochran. Incentive Publications, Inc., Nashville, TN, copyright °1993.

Take-Home Portfolio Questionnaire—Page 1

Student's Name _____ Date_____

Parent's/Caregiver's Name_____

Portfolio Samples 1. _____

2. _____

Parent/caregiver and child complete these questions together.

Portfolio Sample One: _____

Why did you choose this piece? _____

_____

_____

What is your favorite thing about it? _____

_____

_____

What steps did you go through to create and complete it? _____

_____

_____

Portfolio Sample Two: _____

Why did you choose this piece? _____

_____

_____

What do you like about it? _____

_____

_____

Was it hard to complete? Why? _____

_____

_____

What do your portfolio samples tell you about the work you can do? _____

_____

_____

Take-Home Portfolio Questionnaire—Page 2

Parents Answer These Questions Alone

What did you learn about your child's work? _____

_____

_____

_____

_____

What impressed you the most? _____

_____

_____

_____

_____

What questions, if any, do you have? _____

_____

_____

_____

_____

_____

_____

OTHER COMMENTS _____

_____

_____

_____

_____

_____

_____

Parent's/Caregiver's Signature_____ Date_____

Student's Signature _____ Date_____

Parent Questions for Parent Conferencing

Use this form to jot down questions you have about your child's progress in school. Space is provided if you wish to take notes during your parent conference.

Student's Name_____Grade_____ Date_____

Questions	Notes/Comments
Attitude Toward School	

Attitude Toward School

1. What subjects and activities does my child enjoy?

_____

_____

_____

_____

Academic Achievement

2. In what areas is my child doing well?

_____

_____

3. In what areas does my child need help?

_____

_____

4. How is my child's general progress?

_____

_____

Behavior

5. How does my child behave in the classroom?

_____

_____

6. How does my child interact with others?

_____

_____

_____

_____

Other Questions?

_____

_____

_____

_____

_____

BIBLIOGRAPHY

Anderson, Richard C., et al. *Becoming a Nation of Readers: The Report of the Commission on Reading.* Champaign, IL: University of Illinois, Center for the Study of Reading, 1985.

Anthony, Robert J., et al. *Evaluating Literacy: A Perspective for Change.* Portsmouth, NH: Heinemann Educational Books, Inc., 1991.

Batzle, Janine. *Portfolio Assessment and Evaluation.* Cypress, CA: Creative Teaching Press, 1992.

Bauer, Karen and Rosa Drew. *Alternatives to Worksheets.* Cypress, CA: Creative Teaching Press, 1992.

Butler, Andrea. *Guided Reading.* Crystal Lake, IL: Rigby Education, 1988.

——. *Shared Book Experience: An Introduction.* Crystal Lake, IL: Rigby Education, 1987.

Butler, Andrea and Jan Turnbill. *Towards a Reading-Writing Classroom.* Portsmouth, NH: Heinemann Educational Books, Inc., 1987.

Clay, Marie. *The Early Detection of Reading Difficulties.* Portsmouth, NH: Heinemann Educational Books, Inc., 1979.

Cochran, Judith. *Everything You Need To Know To Be a Successful Whole Language Teacher.* Nashville, TN: Incentive Publications, 1993.

——. *Incorporating Literature into the Basal Reading Program.* Nashville, TN: Incentive Publications, 1991.

——. *Insights to Literature, Middle Grades.* Nashville, TN: Incentive Publications, 1990.

——. *Insights to Literature, Primary.* Nashville, TN: Incentive Publications, 1991.

——. *Integrating Science and Literature.* Nashville, TN: Incentive Publications, 1992.

——. *Using Literature To Learn About Children Around the World.* Nashville, TN: Incentive Publications, 1993.

——. *Using Literature To Learn About the First Americans.* Nashville, TN: Incentive Publications, 1993.

——. *What To Do with the Gifted Child.* Nashville, TN: Incentive Publications, 1992.

Comfort, Claudette Hegel. *The Newbery-Caldecott Books in the Classroom.* Nashville, TN: Incentive Publications, 1991.

Cook, Shirley. *Linking Literature and Comprehension: Integrating Literature into Basic Skills Programs.* Nashville, TN: Incentive Publications, Inc., 1992.

———. *Linking Literature with Self-Esteem: Integrating Literature into Basic Skills Programs.* Nashville, TN: Incentive Publications, Inc., 1992

Cook, Shirley and Kathy Carl. *Linking Literature and Writing: Integrating Literature into Basic Skills Programs.* Nashville, TN: Incentive Publications, Inc., 1989.

C.R.E.S.S.T. (The National Center for Research on Evaluation, Standards, and Student Testing). *Portfolio Assessment and High Technology.* Produced by U.S. Department of Education, Office of Educational Research and Improvement, Apple Computer, Inc., 1992. Videocassette.

Eggleton, Jill. *Whole Language Evaluation: Reading, Writing, and Spelling.* Bothell, WA: The Wright Group, 1990.

Eisele, Beverly. *Managing the Whole Language Classroom.* Cypress, CA: Creative Teaching Press, 1991.

Elementary Grades Task Force Report. *It's Elementary!* Sacramento, CA: California Department of Education, 1992.

Elkind, David. *The Hurried Child: Growing Up Too Soon Too Fast.* Reading, MA: Addison-Wesley, 1981.

Fader, Daniel. *The New Hooked on Books.* New York, NY: Berkeley Publishing Corporation, 1982.

Farr, Beverly and Roger. *Integrated Assessment System: Language Arts Performance Assessment.* New York, NY: The Psychological Corporation, HBJ, 1990.

Fehring, Heather and Valerie Thomas. *The Teaching of Spelling.* Crystal Lake, IL: Rigby Education, 1987.

Forte, Imogene. *From A to Z with Books and Me.* Nashville, TN: Incentive Publications, Inc., 1991.

Forte, Imogene and Joy MacKenzie. *Celebrate with Books: Literature-based Whole Language Units for Seasons and Holidays.* Nashville, TN: Incentive Publications, Inc., 1991.

Gentry, J. Richard. *Spel . . . Is a Four-Letter Word.* Portsmouth, NH: Heinemann Educational Books, Inc., 1987.

Goodman, Ken. *What's Whole in Whole Language?* Portsmouth, NH: Heinemann Educational Books, Inc., 1986.

Goodman, Ken, Yetta Goodman, and Wendy Hood, eds. *The Whole Language Evaluation Book.* Portsmouth, NH: Heinemann Educational Books, Inc., 1989.

Hancock, Joelie and Susan Hill, eds. *Literature Based Reading Programs at Work.* Portsmouth, NH: Heinemann Educational Books, Inc., 1988.

Hirsch, E.D., Jr. *Cultural Literacy: What Every American Needs To Know.* Boston: Houghton Mifflin, 1987.

Hornsby, David, Deborah Sukarna and Jo-Ann Parry. *Read On: A Conference Approach to Reading.* Portsmouth, NH: Heinemann Educational Books, Inc., 1988.

Hunter, Madeline. *Increasing Learning Through Effective Practice.* Sacramento, CA: California Elementary Education Association, 1987.

Integrated Assessment System: Understanding Performance Assessment. New York, NY: The Psychological Corporation, 1991.

Jasmine, Julia. *Portfolio Assessment for Your Whole Language Classroom.* Huntington Beach, CA: Teacher Created Materials, Inc., 1992.

McCracken, Robert A. and Marlene J. *Reading Is Only the Tiger's Tail.* Kimberly, British Columbia, Canada: Classroom Publications, 1985.

McCracken, Robert A. and Marlene J. *Spelling Through Phonics.* Winnipeg, Manitoba, Canada: Peguis Publishers, Ltd., 1990.

Manning, Gary and Maryann, eds. *Whole Language: Beliefs and Practices, K-8.* Washington D.C.: National Education Association, 1989.

Modesto City Schools. *Language Arts Performance Assessment, Grades 1-4.* Modesto, CA: Modesto City Schools, 1991.

National Commission on Excellence in Education. *A Nation at Risk: The Imperative for Educational Reform.* Washington, D.C., U.S. Department of Education, 1983.

Newkirk, Thomas and Nancie Atwell, eds. *Understanding Writing: Ways of Observing, Learning, and Teaching.* Portsmouth, NH: Heinemann Educational Books, Inc., 1988.

Parry, Jo-Ann and David Hornsby. *Write On: A Conference Approach to Writing.* Portsmouth, NH: Heinemann Educational Books, Inc., 1989.

Pelphrey, Jo Ann. *Into the Think Tank with Literature.* Nashville, TN: Incentive Publications, Inc., 1992.

Preview CTBS: Comprehensive Tests of Basic Skills, Complete Battery. Fourth Edition. New York, NY: CTB McGraw-Hill, 1989.

Recommended Readings in Literature. Sacramento, CA: California State Department of Education, 1986.

Research about Teaching and Learning. Compiled by the U.S. Department of Education. Washington, D.C., U.S. Department of Education, 1986.

Routman, Regie. *Invitations: Changing as Teachers and Learners, K–12.* Portsmouth, NH: Heinemann Educational Books, Inc., 1991.

Sonoma Valley Unified School District. *If You're Gonna Teach Literature, You Gotta Have This Book.* Sonoma, CA: Sonoma Valley Unified School District, 1989.

Stewig, John. *Read to Write.* New York, NY: Richard C. Owen Publishers, Inc., 1980.

Student Essays Illustrating the CAP Rhetorical Effectiveness Scoring System. Sacramento, CA: California State Department of Education, 1989.

Trelease, Jim. *The New Read-Aloud Handbook.* New York, NY: Penguin, 1989.

Wells, Gordon. *The Meaning Makers: Children Learning Language and Using Language To Learn.* Portsmouth, NH: Heinemann Educational Books, Inc., 1986.